DOES PRIVILEGE PREVAIL?

CONSTITUTIONALISM
AND DEMOCRACY

Gregg Ivers and
Kevin T. McGuire,
Editors

Does Privilege Prevail?

LITIGATION IN HIGH COURTS
ACROSS THE GLOBE

Stacia L. Haynie, Kirk A. Randazzo,
and Reginald S. Sheehan

University of Virginia Press | Charlottesville and London

The University of Virginia Press is situated on the traditional lands of the Monacan Nation, and the Commonwealth of Virginia was and is home to many other Indigenous people. We pay our respect to all of them, past and present. We also honor the enslaved African and African American people who built the University of Virginia, and we recognize their descendants. We commit to fostering voices from these communities through our publications and to deepening our collective understanding of their histories and contributions.

University of Virginia Press
© 2024 by the Rector and Visitors of the University of Virginia
All rights reserved
Printed in the United States of America on acid-free paper

First published 2024

9 8 7 6 5 4 3 2 1

Library of Congress Cataloging-in-Publication Data

Names: Haynie, Stacia L., author. | Randazzo, Kirk A., author. | Sheehan, Reginald S., author.
Title: Does privilege prevail? : litigation in high courts across the globe / Stacia L. Haynie, Kirk A. Randazzo, and Reginald S. Sheehan.
Description: Charlottesville : University of Virginia Press, 2024. | Series: Constitutionalism and democracy | Includes bibliographical references and index.
Identifiers: LCCN 2023049647 (print) | LCCN 2023049648 (ebook) | ISBN 9780813951102 (cloth) | ISBN 9780813951119 (paperback) | ISBN 9780813951126 (ebook)
Subjects: LCSH: Courts of last resort. | Judicial process. | Judicial power. | Constitutional law.
Classification: LCC K2123 .H39 2024 (print) | LCC K2123 (ebook) | DDC 347/.03553—dc23/eng/20231024
LC record available at https://lccn.loc.gov/2023049647
LC ebook record available at https://lccn.loc.gov/2023049648

Cover art: Map from the P. J. Mode collection of persuasive cartography, #8548, Division of Rare and Manuscript Collections, Cornell University Library; obverse of 1967 British penny.

Cover design: Kelley Galbreath

CONTENTS

ACKNOWLEDGMENTS

We are grateful to the National Science Foundation, to our own universities, to our colleagues, to the many judges, lawyers, advocates, and journalists who worked with us, to the scores of undergraduate and graduate students who helped to code, enter, and clean the data, and especially to our families, who supported this project, including during our months away for fieldwork. However, no two individuals have been more instrumental in seeing this project to fruition than C. Neal Tate and Donald R. Songer. Stacy was fortunate enough to have Neal as her PhD adviser; Reggie had Don as his PhD adviser, and Don's influence extended to Kirk, who was advised by Reggie. Kirk also had the wonderful opportunity of working with Don as a student and later as a colleague at the University of South Carolina.

Neal began the effort to move the study of law and courts beyond the borders of the United States early in his career. Indeed, his dissertation on the Philippine Supreme Court was pathbreaking for its time. Neal rightly asserted that theories built and tested only for the US Supreme Court were limited in helping us understand judicial behavior generally. He paved the way for comparative judicial scholars to occupy critical and important intellectual space in the discipline. Don became the preeminent scholar of the US courts of appeal and an expert on building original multiuser data sets. His intellectual breadth was as impressive as it was unflagging. Large swaths of the scholarly work in the field are the products of Don's or his intellectual progeny's thinking. Stacy and Reggie were each privileged to have partnered with Neal and Don to create the National High Courts Database with funding from the National Science Foundation. We lost these two amazing scholars too early in their lives; it was a personal loss for the three of us and a significant professional loss for the discipline. In the years since their passing, we made a commitment to complete this book not just because we believed it would be an important contribution to the field but because our mentors would have expected nothing less. Neal and Don were the driving force behind the intellectual curiosity that has prompted not just this book but the work of each of us as scholars and individuals. As we think of Neal and Don, we can only repeat the inimitable words of Stephen Schwartz: "Because I knew you, I have been changed for good."

DOES PRIVILEGE PREVAIL?

Introduction

There are many pleasant fictions of the law in constant operation, but there is not one so pleasant or practically humorous as that which supposes every man to be of equal value in its impartial eye, and the benefits of all laws to be equally attainable by all men, without the smallest reference to the furniture of their pockets.

— Charles Dickens, *Nicholas Nickleby*

LITIGATION IS AN adversarial process in which one party seeks to prevail over another to resolve a conflict. These conflicts arise because one of the litigants to the conflict believes that the rules have been breached. Rules arise because societies reach some agreement as to the accepted norms of behavior. If conflicts arise over what does or does not conform to the rules, some entity must have the designated authority to resolve the disputes. Absent such authority, the parties will persist in conflict or the conflict may escalate to violence or other coercive ends. Either alternative decreases the stability and predictability of social interactions. By articulating expectations through written rules and by authorizing an arbiter to clarify the rules, communities hope to establish a structure that will increase stability and peacefully perpetuate society.

For this rule of law to emerge, society broadly must agree that the legal system is an acceptable avenue for resolving the dispute. Because disputes inevitably benefit one party over another, the legitimacy of the process, or the belief in the legitimacy of the process, facilitates the capacity of the losing party to accept the arbiter's decision. The litigants believe that the arbiter—or the judge—applies the law impartially and equitably to the facts. The rule of law emerges and persists because the losing party accepts the legitimacy of the legal system and their loss within it.

We seek to comprehensively evaluate what scholars know and do not know about winning and losing in courts of law. In doing so, we evaluate prior research to determine the characteristics and conditions that affect who wins and who loses. While we are not the first to seek to understand the underlying dimensions of court decisions, much prior research has focused on the US courts or, when the focus has turned elsewhere, on the courts of single nations. These efforts ground our understanding of the effect of a variety of potential sources of influence on litigation outcomes, but they do not provide the comparative advantage that comes from studying multiple countries across a significant span of time. Our study is the first truly comparative empirical analysis to fill that gap. Our evaluation of decades of decisions of high courts in multiple countries that vary in political, economic, and legal organization provides the first rigorous and systematic analysis of litigation outcomes. Moreover, it affords us greater confidence in the generalizability of our findings. We also offer our thoughts about the consequences of our findings for the perceived legitimacy of courts and the persistence of the rule of law.

As individuals begin to organize their interactions through structured rules, governments emerge designated to establish guidelines over "who gets what, when, how" (Lasswell 1958). Institutions emerge that translate those decisions into concrete policies. Inevitably, conflicts emerge over the distribution of resources, the violations of rules or norms, the processes that drive the distributions and the punishments, and so on. Adjudicative bodies are established specifically to resolve these disputes. Courts, and the judges who constitute them, serve as one of the political institutions responsible for the authoritative allocation of values (Easton 1965). These bodies are established to apply the rules to the facts of the disputes brought before them and thus to determine winners and losers.

Courts are obviously political bodies by the very nature of their structure and function. The function of courts as allocators of gains and losses differs at the trial and appellate levels. For trial courts, resolution of a conflict may affect only the parties directly in dispute. A couple seeking a divorce, a business owner involved in a contract settlement, or a person entering a plea bargain in a criminal case are specific individuals with specific disagreements that are ultimately decided by the designated authority. For appellate courts, of course, the rulings serve as statements that clarify the relationship of the law to individual interactions. These statements, or judicial choices, serve as policies that are broadly applicable to social intercourse.

Because these decisions are important in establishing an avenue to resolve conflicts, and further, are important as policy constructs for society at large, understanding these choices is critical if we are to understand judges, judging, and the rule of law. Judicial decisions allocate political, social, and economic resources in society. Appellate courts in particular serve as one component of the "power filter" (Dhavan 1985, 26). By analyzing the highest appellate courts in a society, we can examine the relationship between the regime's authoritative allocation of the values through "law" and the judiciary's response in its establishment of the "rule of law" through its determinations of who wins and who loses. The legitimacy of the legal system requires judges to balance their role as political actors with preserving the perception of mechanical jurisprudence. Since the emergence of the legal realist school of thought, scholars have rejected a mechanistic understanding of the legal process and have sought to understand external factors that affect legal decisions.

Marc Galanter's classic work provides the framework for why the law would favor more powerful litigants—those he terms the "haves"—relative to those who are less powerful—the "have-nots" (1974). Galanter argues that a number of advantages enjoyed by the haves skew success rates in their favor. First, he argues that those who utilize the courts repetitively (repeat players) are more likely to succeed than those who access the courts rarely or singularly (one-shotters). Among the advantages enjoyed by repeat players are substantial resources that allow them to either develop or secure experienced legal talent and specialists. Indeed, those repeat players who enjoy in-house counsel or ongoing relationships with particular expertise "enjoy economies of scale" that lower the cost of any single case. In addition, they are able to foster ongoing relationships with "institutional incumbents." Knowing the court's personnel, including judges and clerks, facilitates informal relationships that Galanter argues inevitably benefit the repeat players. Repeat players also enjoy the ability to "adopt a minimax strategy," one in which the repeat player minimizes the possibility of a maximum loss. Repeat players can engage in litigation knowing some losses are inevitable when risk assessment allows maximum gains over the long haul (Galanter 1974, 98–100, passim).

Additionally, greater resources allow repeat players to engage in long-term strategies to shape the rules in their favor, rather than focus on a single outcome. Because one-shotters have only the single case to concern them, they must play the hand they are dealt rather than settle a case that may be brought before a less sympathetic court or whose facts are not entirely favorable. Repeat players, on the other hand, can settle a case that they wish to avoid as potentially setting a negative precedent or can drag the litigation out through costly procedures and rules, procedures and rules that are influenced by repeat players in the first place. Albiston (1999, 2003) argues that one-shotters who settle their claim provide an important tactical benefit to the haves. If a one-shotter gains a favorable settlement, the common law will remain silent on the individual right that was vindicated by the repeat players' positive response to the claim. Recognizing this, repeat players will settle those cases that could lead to more favorable rules for one-shotters. Albiston claims that this creates a "paradox of losing by winning" in which for "one-shot players claiming individual rights, success comes at the price of silence in the historical record of the common law. Thus, once again, the haves come out ahead" (Albiston 1999, 906).

Galanter particularly emphasizes the importance of skilled representation in courts of law—an advantage more readily available to repeat players, but an advantage that can temper the likelihood of an outcome favorable to the have-nots if less powerful litigants are able to secure skilled attorneys. Indeed, Galanter (1974) sees lawyers themselves as repeat players who could potentially "equalize the parties" but are much more likely to be retained by repeat players, given the general organization of the legal profession (114). Repeat players are more likely to access specialists and more likely to enjoy loyalty from the practitioners with whom they interact more regularly than are one-shotters. Lawyers who cater to one-shotters tend to make up the "lower echelons" of the profession; they are drawn from lower socioeconomic strata, attend less notable law schools, practice in solo firms, and have lower prestige in the profession (Galanter 1974, 113–17; see also Heinz and Lauman 1982). Galanter also notes that lawyers who represent one-shotters tend to have difficulty mobilizing large numbers of plaintiffs because of ethical barriers forbidding solicitation and because of low information among one-shotters who may have claims. The resulting seriatim interaction with differing individuals leads to an "uncreative brand of legal services." Galanter further argues that lawyers, unlike corporations, cannot sacrifice one case to win cases further down the line. A lawyer cannot view a series of one-shotter clients "as if they constituted a single RP." Thus, while Galanter concedes that attorneys theoretically could counterbalance the advantages of the haves, they are constrained by the organization and the logistics of the bar (117–19).

Galanter also suggests that the institutional features of the legal system perpetuate the power of repeat players. He particularly notes that courts are passive and must be mobilized by litigants who have the resources and skill sets to navigate the costly and time-consuming processes involved in litigation. Repeat players are more likely to have such resources available. Moreover, courts manage far more claims than could ever be individually adjudicated, creating pressure to settle rather than litigate, pressure that Galanter argues benefits repeat players (119–22).

Finally, Galanter notes the rules themselves favor the dominant interests in society. He argues it is not just that the rules reflect the preferences of the powerful but that the development of the rules over time reflects the class-based nature of society and helps "protect and promote the tangible interests of organized and influential groups." It is also the case that the rules themselves are complex and difficult to navigate (or can be made to be so, as Galanter notes) absent significant resources (123–24).

Galanter specifically argues that repeat players are more likely to win cases in appellate courts — our venue of analysis. Because repeat players are focused on longer-term strategies, they are most likely to appeal those cases for which they expect a favorable decision establishing precedent that will be beneficial to future litigation. Conversely, they will settle those cases where they fear an adverse outcome that could negatively affect their interests not merely in the case at bar but, more critically, in the longer term. Galanter suggests the increased likelihood of repeat players in appellate courts is prompted by their ability "to trigger promising cases" and avoid the "unpromising ones." Indeed, Galanter argues that litigants before courts of law "are treated as if they were equally endowed with economic resources, investigative opportunities and legal skills. Where, as is usually the case, they are not, the broader the delegation to the parties, the greater the advantage conferred on the wealthier, more experienced and better organized party" (120).

In sum, Galanter provides a theoretical foundation for why, as Rousseau (1768) argued more than two hundred years before, the universal spirit of the law will favor the strong, and that this "inconveniency is inevitable, and without exception" (46). The dominance enjoyed by the haves results from the advantages that "interlock, reinforcing and shielding" (Galanter 1974, 124) the powerful, ensuring that they "have more law" (Black 1976, 17).

We find Galanter's theoretical arguments compelling, and we are not alone. Hundreds of scholars before us have been similarly intrigued by his arguments and have sought to test them empirically. Before we test Galanter's thesis ourselves, we investigate those who have previously assessed his theoretical framework. In chapter 1 we provide the most comprehensive evaluation to date of the scholarship testing Galanter's theory in in the American legal context. More recently, and particularly relevant for our comparative analysis, scholars have moved beyond the boundaries of the US to test Galanter's thesis across the globe. We provide the most extensive review to date of these studies in chapter 2. Combined, chapters 1 and 2 represent an important assessment of the scholarly work analyzing Galanter's iconic article in the decades that followed its reception by the discipline. In chapter 3 we assess winners and losers across different categories of litigants and different issue categories. We are interested in whether repeat players are advantaged in high court outcomes when challenging or challenged by one-shotters.[1] We are also able to test the ability of the haves, or those with greater resources, to prevail over those with fewer resources, the have-nots. In chapter 4 we focus specifically on the ultimate repeat player, the government, by analyzing litigation outcomes for both national and subnational governments across different combinations of parties and legal issues. Chapter 5 provides a comprehensive model of litigation outcomes that allows us to control for differences in political and economic variation, as well as variation in the legal systems across the countries we study. This analysis is the first ever to utilize comparative empirical models to assess Galanter's thesis across multiple high courts and decades of their decisions. Chapters 3, 4, and 5 each begin with a discussion of cases drawn from the database. While we are interested in the aggregate outcomes across the courts we study, each case in the database involves real people with real conflicts seeking resolution. We present these case studies to provide both context and examples of types of one-shotters and repeat players frequently represented in the data.

The data utilized in our analyses are drawn from the National High Courts Database, which includes over 15,000 decisions from the highest courts of appeal in Australia, Canada, the United Kingdom, South Africa, India, and the Philippines from 1970 to 2000.[2] We discuss the data set in more detail in chapter 3, but these countries share a common law heritage while exhibiting critical differences in the political, social, and economic criteria essential for comparative inquiry.

In chapter 6 we offer concluding thoughts about the results and their implications for the rule of law. If Dickens is correct that equality before the law is merely a fiction, are there consequences for democracy and the rule of law? If the legitimacy of courts rests on the perceived—if not actual—impartiality of their rulings, what happens if the system is inevitably tilted toward those with more furniture in their pockets? What can courts do to balance the scales of justice if Galanter is correct that the haves inevitably come out ahead? Testing Galanter's thesis is a critical first step toward answering that question.

1 | Party Capability Theory in the United States

A GREAT DEAL of research has focused on what affects the ability of one litigant to succeed in a court of law and another to fail. This chapter provides a comprehensive review of the literature by scholars who have tested Galanter's haves versus have-nots and repeat players versus one-shotters thesis in the American context. We focus on research that confirms the advantage of repeat players, the circumstances that increase the likelihood of the have-nots prevailing, and the advantages that lawyers and interest groups provide. We also review research assessing the impact of ideology and the advantages that accrue to a special category of repeat player, the government.

Advantage Repeat Players

Galanter (1974) argues that the basic architecture of the American legal system ensures that those parties with greater capabilities will prevail in courts of law. According to his party capability theory, repeat players who are in court frequently have greater experience and expertise, can settle cases that may be unfavorable to their long-term interests, can secure the best legal talent, are familiar with the institutional incumbents, and even shape the rules of the game. One-shotters, he says, enjoy none of these benefits. One-shotters are typically in court only once, are concerned only about the case at hand, are not familiar with the legal terrain, and, as a result of these factors, typically lose. Repeat players such as businesses, associations, and especially the government succeed more often than do one-shotters, who are typically individuals. Galanter is careful not to equate the haves with repeat players and the have-nots with one-shotters. He recognizes that there can be rich and powerful one-shotters, for example wealthy individuals who may be criminal defendants, but they are the exception to the rule. He argues that repeat players in the American context are "larger, richer and more powerful" than the one-shotters (103).

Galanter's thesis threw down a theoretical gauntlet to scholars of judicial politics, a gauntlet that was picked up by empirical researchers interested in the validity of his claims. Initial efforts focused on the US legal system. Among the first to test his claims empirically was Galanter himself, with data collected in prior studies. Galanter (1975) utilized data collected for civil courts of general jurisdiction in several US counties (Owen 1971; Wanner 1974); claims before the justice of the peace in Arizona courts (Bruff 1973); and small claims courts in California (Moulton 1969; Pagter, McCloskey, and Renis 1964), Illinois (Smith 1970), Massachusetts (Small Claims Study Group 1972), and Ohio (Hollingsworth, Feldman, and Clark 1974), among others.

In Galanter's (1975) meta-analysis of these data, he finds, with only a few exceptions, patterns that meet his expectations. Repeat players, which he operationalizes as "organizations," challenging one-shotters, which he operationalizes as individuals, are the modal category among the four cells of Galanter's typology (repeat player versus repeat player, one-shotter versus one-shotter, one-shotter versus repeat player, and repeat player versus one-shotter). In evaluating winners and losers, Galanter again confirms his hypotheses that repeat players are the most likely to succeed. He finds that "litigation is undertaken mainly by organizations" and that "they enjoy greater success at it" (359–60). In the few jurisdictions that do not meet the expected pattern, Galanter hypothesizes that differences in legal services may explain the variation from his hypothesized outcomes, but he recognizes that his assertion awaits further empirical testing. The complexity of the legal system, he argues, delivers persistent benefits to repeat players, though he concedes that ascribing a party the label of "organization" or "individual" overlaps with distinctions of "wealthy" and "poor," at least in the American context (363).

Although not explicitly testing Galanter's repeat player thesis, Grossman and Sarat (1975) evaluate the relationship between socioeconomic factors and civil cases per 100,000 population in US federal district courts, as well as the effect of socioeconomic factors on legal activity as measured by lawyers per 100,000 population. They find underlying advantages for the powerful in their analysis, concluding that their results "reinforce the common wisdom that the legal system is oriented strongly toward the service of wealth and property. As a whole, our findings tend to confirm the hypothesized cross-sectional relationships between legal activity, on the one hand, and affluence and industrialization on the other" (33).

Using data from trials in Chicago from 1971 and 1972, Lizotte (1978) evaluates a special category of repeat player versus one-shotter: the prosecutor and the criminal defendant. Lizotte finds there is "gross inequality" in sentencing that is directly affected by race and lower occupational status, and that these socioeconomic factors also affect sentencing through their indirect effect on the ability to make bail (577). Those defendants with resources reap lighter sentences or serve no time at all. Lizotte's findings confirm Galanter's expectations in that even among one-shotters, those with presumably greater resources fare better in litigation outcomes.

In studying 150 years of civil litigation (1820–1970) in the trial courts of St. Louis, Missouri, McIntosh (1980–81) finds that over time, tort cases increased from fewer than 10 percent of the docket to more than 30 percent. Family law cases increased as well. These litigants occupy the one-shotter versus one-shotter category, which Galanter suggests is really "pseudo-litigation" in which the parties essentially have agreed to the settlement, and the law is invoked in an instrumental way to achieve resolution of the conflict (Galanter 1974, 108). Interestingly, McIntosh notes that such collusive divorce cases initially were prohibited by the legislature, which under the 1845 statute required adversary action with presentation of evidence and testimony from persons knowledgeable of the parties. Defendants found "guilty" of marital fault were required to forfeit the ability to remarry for five years. Corresponding to shifting mores concerning divorce, the adversarial nature of the process evolved into the pro forma procedure Galanter anticipates.

Subsequent analysis by McIntosh (1985) finds that individuals were most likely to be plaintiffs across the 150 years, and corporations were most likely to be defendants. Contrary to Galanter's expectations, McIntosh finds that individuals were the predominant plaintiff in debt collection, property, and tort liability cases, while wholesale and retail merchants were frequently defendants during the time frame. Organizations were the primary plaintiff (against other organizations) in contract disputes.

In their study of state supreme court decisions, Wheeler et al. (1987) find persistent, if not overwhelming, advantages for the haves. The advantage of repeat players is "generally small" but does persist across issues and time. The authors suggest that three primary factors drive the results: (1) the law itself favors the haves; (2) judges favor the haves; and (3) litigation skill sets favor the haves. Nonetheless, the authors conclude that the "'little guys' could and did receive justice in the state supreme courts, at least in the sense of winning almost half of the time" (443). As the law develops, the interaction of repeat players and one-shotters can vary. Indeed, if repeat players are engaging in long-term legal strategies and specifically are working to shape the rules to their advantage, we should anticipate greater success on their part over time.

Hamzehzadeh (2010) finds exactly this in his study of Walmart, an iconic example of the repeat player. He suggests that Walmart was the equivalent of a one-shotter in the early years of its existence. It had only two forays into the legal system—two cases in the 1960s and 1970s—and lost both. While the company was involved with slightly more litigation in the 1980s, its success reflects that of a one-shotter (50 percent) rather than that expected of a repeat player. However, as the company became the prototypical repeat player in the 1990s its success rate climbed concomitantly to 67 percent and to 66 percent in the 2000s. Hamzehzadeh also argues that the increasing success was attributable to favorable rule changes and court precedents. The results provide considerable support, at least in this case study, that the company succeeds both as a repeat player in court and as a repeat player playing for the rules.

Henderson and Eisenberg's (1990) study of products liability cases finds significant support for Galanter's assertion that the haves come out ahead. Their analysis of over 200,000 federal civil claims lends strong support to party capability theory. Corporations won over 90 percent of cases in which they sued an individual, whereas individuals won only 50 percent of the time.

A study of Baltimore's specialized rent court finds that the haves prevail over the have-nots on a consistent basis (Bezdek 1992). A single judge can dispose of well over 2,000 cases in any single day, and more than 195,000 cases for summary ejectment are filed by landlords against their tenants each year. Supporting Galanter's premise, landlords, as repeat players, were almost always the plaintiff and prevailed 67 percent of the time; the tenant was almost always the defendant and lost more frequently. Moreover, in those cases in which the tenant brought a claim of inhabitability, the landlord avoided damages or rent abatement in 98 percent of cases. Bezdek argues that the conjunction of two factors, "being black and being poor," is critical to understanding the success of the landlord haves over the tenant have-nots (603).

In a study of business litigation among several thousand US corporations, Dunworth and Rogers (1996) find that the volume of cases grew during the 1970s and 1980s in federal courts but declined in the later years of the analysis; moreover, the data reveal that business-related litigation was dominated by a very small number of what Dunworth and Rogers refer to as "mega-litigants," those who account for the bulk of litigation activity. This is especially true in tort litigation, where the trend line is flat or declining over the several decades they study. More critically, "big business wins overwhelmingly, as plaintiff and defendant, in cases that involve it" (502). While we should not be surprised that corporations dominate business litigation, the results suggest that there are exceptionally powerful repeat players who are particularly advantaged in the legal system.

Gross's (1996) study of litigation in California's superior trial courts from 1985 to 1986, however, suggests that the haves are not significantly advantaged. He finds that over 70 percent of the trials involved personal injury cases and that individuals were the primary plaintiff in more than 90 percent of cases. His evaluation of outcomes shows that individuals won about 50 percent of the time. This echoes the findings of Henderson and Eisenberg (1990) and indicates that organizations, the modal category of defendants, are perhaps more willing to risk trial than Galanter anticipated. Gross suggests that one reason both individuals and organizations may be willing to continue to trial is that neither the plaintiff, for whom the contingency fee limits the resources required, nor the defendant, for whom insurance minimizes cost, is financing the litigation.

Thus one-shotters can benefit from strategic alliances with repeat players. Repeat players' support of individual litigants may temper the anticipated advantage of repeat players over one-shotters as plaintiffs. Gross suggests that such an alliance may be driven by the long-term interests of the repeat players, again, who play for the rules. Gross also notes that the funding mechanisms for litigation are a critical driver in the settlement process. In their study of cases brought by Indigenous peoples before state supreme courts, Reid and Curry (2021) find no benefit for appellants supported by the federal government, the ultimate repeat player. Indigenous litigants who challenge "resource-rich opponents" are less likely to win. However, their likelihood of success increases in states where Indigenous peoples make up a higher percentage of the population.

Oppenheimer's (2003) study of jury verdicts in California employment discrimination cases finds that judges and juries appear skeptical of race- and sex-based employment discrimination claims. Oppenheimer finds lower success rates for women and minorities in sex-, race-, and age-based discrimination cases than for male and white plaintiffs. Overall statistics suggest a disadvantage for have-nots among jurors.

Cheit and Gersen (2000) study business litigation (businesses suing businesses) in the Rhode Island Superior Court from 1987 to 1988 and find that particularly large businesses are repeat players in litigation and that litigants in major industry groups are fairly split between plaintiffs and defendants. The authors argue that this makes playing for the rules a less attractive strategy for some issue categories. For example, if the repeat players play for the rules and structure a pro-defendant regime, but then are almost as likely to be a plaintiff as a defendant, they are less likely to engage in rules that favor the plaintiff over the defendant or vice versa. Their results suggest that under certain con-straints (those sectors of the litigation game where repeat players initiate the suit as often as they defend themselves in one), repeat players face a similar single outcome focus as one-shotters.

Other studies of jury verdicts also find a compelling pro-defendant bias in civil cases. A study of Ohio jury verdicts from 1984 to 1996 finds that filings for product liability cases decreased by almost two-thirds over the time period and that the likelihood of recovery and the size of the verdict did not increase over this time frame; moreover, not a single award for punitive damages was recorded. Despite the empirical evidence, repeat players were able to pass tort reform in Ohio in 1996 that limited the ability of parties to recover damages. Repeat players "played for the rules" so that even if litigants were successful, the award would be limited (Merritt and Barry 1999).

In their study of civil jury verdicts in Alabama from 2002 to 2008, Dumas and Haynie (2012) find that repeat players have greater success. However, in-dividuals who bring their cases before more liberal communities and com-munities in the lower socioeconomic strata have a greater likelihood of suc-ceeding than individuals whose litigation is determined by juries drawn from populations that do not reflect these characteristics.

Hadfield's (2005) analysis of federal civil trial courts from 1970 to 2000 finds that organizational plaintiffs, whether suing other organizations or indi-viduals, are much more likely to settle cases than are individuals. He suggests that this higher settlement rate "may suggest that organizational plaintiffs are less interested in rule change or precedent than individual plaintiffs" (1319). The combination of these two trends, Hadfield argues, may "reflect an asym-metry in access to legal resources" (1322), an imbalance Galanter also argues that advantages the haves in litigation outcomes.

Edelman et al. (2011) not only analyze the winner and loser in terms of the verdict but also evaluate the legal opinions in federal employment discrimi-nation claims. The authors argue that judges are deferential to formal policies and organizational structures that portend the potential of protection against discrimination. These decisions reflected the recent precedent of the US Su-preme Court in *Wal-Mart Stores, Inc. v. Dukes* (2011) in which the justices, in a 5–4 decision along ideological lines, recognized that Walmart had a policy in place that forbade employment discrimination and gave much less weight to the fact that it appeared to have little impact on actual gender discrimination in the company. Deference to these formal organizational policies, the authors argue, co-opts the legal system, creating an endogenous influence that theoretically should remain exogenous.

The results of an analysis of the district courts of Maryland, Georgia, and Pennsylvania seem to support the findings of Edelman et al. (2011). Brown (2011) explores the settlement rates across employment discrimination, tort, and contract cases for 2007 and 2008 and finds greater success on the part of repeat players, especially when discrimination and tort cases are compared to contract cases. Brown also finds variation in settlement rates over time and across jurisdictions.

Focusing on a random sample of almost 2,000 published opinions of the supreme courts of Alabama, Kansas, New Jersey, South Dakota, and West Virginia from 1975, 1980, 1985, and 1990, Farole (1999) attempts to test Galanter's thesis for state appeal courts. He finds that individuals won against businesses about 45 percent of the time, while businesses fared only slightly better when challenging individuals, winning 47 percent of the time. Criminal defendants had higher success rates against local governments (40 percent success rate) compared to state governments (33 percent success rate), but only a one in three chance of success overall. While repeat players do appear advantaged over one-shotters, "the systematic differences between businesses and individuals predicted by Galanter (1974) simply do not appear" (Farole 1999, 1054).

Rather than evaluating litigation outcomes, Brace and Hall (2001) explore the repeat player advantage in agenda setting for state high courts. Their research finds that docket space for cases involving the haves versus the have-nots is affected by court professionalism, the ideology of both the public and the judges, and a higher number of lawyers per capita, at least for cases where amicus participation was present, their unit of analysis. Have-nots fared better among courts in more liberal states with higher professionalism that were staffed by more liberal judges.

To what extent do the haves exacerbate social, political, and economic inequality through litigation before state supreme courts? Gibson and Nelson (2021) find that the answer is a "mild" yes. In their study of 6,000 cases involving issues of inequality before state high courts in all fifty states from 1990 to 2015, the haves succeeded in 55–59 percent of cases. While clearly succeeding more often than not, the results do not suggest a monolithic advantage for those with greater resources.

Baker (2001) finds that liability insurance, which funds litigation and settlement for policyholders, presents a new complication for Galanter's model.

Baker argues that in tort claims, the plaintiff's lawyer will frame the case to maximize the likelihood of the insurance policy providing a benefit, and the defendant's lawyer cooperates to ensure that only the insurer pays ("new money," as Baker terms it), and not the defendant. This strategy allows both the plaintiff and the defendant to rely on a third-party repeat player, the insurance company, to cover the costs. Baker's logic rests on truly one-shot defendants who do not intend to dip into the insurance well on a repeated basis.

Eisenberg and Farber (1997) evaluate risk for litigants through a rational choice model that envisions trial as a function of the likelihood of losing, the potential damages that could be awarded, and the costs of litigation to the plaintiff and defendant. Plaintiffs, they argue, have greater dispersion in their litigation cost motivations and therefore have more ability to litigate or not, whereas corporations are constrained by their profit motive. As a result, they expect, and they find, that individual plaintiffs have a higher trial rate and a lower win rate than do corporations. Thus "market discipline" constrains corporations sufficiently to ensure greater success for those cases that reach trial, and settlements flow from those cases perceived at greater risk for loss (597). Testing the model on cases filed in federal diversity jurisdiction cases in US district courts from 1986 to 1994, cases that by definition involve more than $50,000, the authors find that individuals have higher trial rates and lower win rates, as predicted. This is especially true when individuals are sued by corporations, which are successful in those litigant interactions 90 percent of the time; conversely, when individuals sue corporations, the success is 50 percent. This also supports Galanter's theoretical structure of the one-shotter versus repeat player interaction.

Studies of the US courts of appeal find that the haves come out ahead. In their study of decisions of the courts of appeal from 1925 to 1988, Songer, Sheehan, and Haire (2003) note that individuals lost more than 60 percent of the time and businesses succeeded about half the time. This pattern was especially strong for those interactions where repeat players faced one-shotters and vice versa. Repeat players exhibit a pattern of success that endures over a half century of litigation, suggesting a more stable advantage than other longitudinal studies.

Lindquist, Martinek, and Hettinger (2007) study a subset of the decisions of the US courts of appeal—decisions with mixed outcomes. The authors find, among other things, that with a repeat player versus repeat player interaction, a decision confirming in part and reversing in part is more likely. They suggest that this is the logical result of two parties with equal, or equally high, capabilities.[1]

Galanter's thesis also explores a continuum of options for conflict resolution in the legal system, with trial at one end and negotiation between parties at the other.[2] Along the continuum are a variety of unofficial as well as official settlement processes.[3] Galanter (1974) does not see these alternatives as necessarily competing or opposed to the values and norms in the formal legal system. Galanter suggests that it is the distance from the official system, which is dominated by the "upper lawyers"; Galanter sees the dominance of repeat players and organizations permeating the majority of the "massive 'legal' iceberg" (134). One piece of the legal iceberg responsible for resolving conflicts is arbitration.

A number of authors have evaluated legal settlements along Galanter's continuum, including alternative dispute resolution processes such as arbitration. In an analysis of arbitration awards under the American Arbitration Association's Commercial and Employment Arbitration rules from 1993 to 1994, Bingham (1997, 1998) finds that employees have much lower success rates in cases involving repeat player employers. She also discovers that even among the one-shotter plaintiffs, who are by far the majority, plaintiffs who enjoy higher-status occupations are more likely to prevail. Bingham finds that "white-collar employees have systematically superior outcomes to blue-collar or pink-collar employees" (1997, 213). Thus, while individuals overall may fare less well, even among one-shotters, those with presumed greater resources— such as white-collar executives—are more likely to succeed than those with fewer resources.

Extensions of Bingham's studies of arbitration outcomes find that the elimination of class action lawsuits has created "extreme repeat players" who are advantaged because of repeated appearances (Horton and Chandrasekher 2015) or repeat players who have appeared previously before an arbitrator (Chandrasekher and Horton 2019; Colvin 2011; Colvin and Gough 2015; Horton and Chandrasekher 2016). This advantage holds regardless of whether the "extreme repeat player" is the plaintiff or respondent. However, Feuille (1997) finds that claimants in arbitration cases where unions are present win about 50 percent of the time. Those plaintiffs, including individuals who enjoy the resources that unions can bring to bear, such as experience, legal talent, and financial resources, have a greater likelihood of winning.[4]

Menkel-Meadow (1999) argues that repeat players have co-opted the arbitration system by coercing customers and clients into mandatory arbitration clauses in their contracts. Repeat players are able to structure the rules of the game through the articulation of contracts in ways that benefit them in these alternative judicial systems. Repeat players have been able "to control the forum, decisionmaker, and rules in order to maximize outcomes" (48). As Galanter argues is the case for formal adjudicative systems, repeat players have played for the rules in alternative ones as well.

Hoffmann (2008) also assesses an alternative to the formal legal system, focusing the analysis on employment disputes. Utilizing a typology that categorizes workers into those with official and unofficial power, Hoffmann finds that those employees with some level of official power—the "have-somes"—are able to access the formal procedures offered by the business to address concerns. The have-nots are more likely either to cope individually with the concern motivating their grievance or to quit. Ultimately, the more powerful have-nots strategically exploit the alternatives available to them to resolve workplace conflicts. Nonetheless, as Hoffmann notes, "management is the ultimate have in the employment-dispute context" and "the advantages of the repeat-player management are evident" (64).

The District of Columbia's private sector workers' compensation system similarly assesses workplace injury claims via informal conference proceedings. Jones (2021) analyzes a random sample of claims appealed to the Compensation Review Board from 2005 to 2019. Despite "distinct advantages built into the architecture of the system," which include a "presumption of compensability" for the injured worker (2), the haves retain an advantage. The author finds that the Compensation Review Board misapplies the "presumption of compensability" to the benefit of the repeat player employers, who "still come out ahead" (3).

Another area of the puzzle evaluated by scholars involves tax audits. Such audits are not litigation, in the sense that there is no case at bar, but they do provide a potential precursor to repeat player litigation should the audit establish rules that are detrimental to repeat players. Audits also include similar legal processes: a valued end or claim, a resistance to the claim, and the use of a specific institution to resolve the dispute (Friedman 1989, 18). In their evaluation of tax audits, Kinsey and Stalans (1999, 2003) find that taxpayers with higher-prestige occupations and small business owners fare better than others. Kinsey and Stalans suggest that these groups have another resource available to them, cultural capital, that is not available or is less available to the have-nots. More critically, they are more likely to introduce a tax practitioner into the audit process. The repeat player tax practitioner tends to benefit the one-shotter individual taxpayer. The advantage of the haves extends more broadly to the initial decision to conduct the audits. Howard (2001) finds that wealthier taxpayers can play for the rules to ensure fewer audits of those with more resources.

In an evaluation of congressional election disputes from 2006 to 2012, repeat players (political parties, interest groups, and incumbent campaigns) were advantaged over one-shotters (individuals and challenger campaigns) in allegations of campaign finance infractions (Lochner et al. 2020). Third-party monitors with greater experience and resources are also more successful than their less experienced counterparts.

Research also suggests that winning in court, or in alternative conflict resolution processes, is not the end of the story. Cartwright (1975) argues that the judicial decision is not always the end of the conflict. If an individual wins in the lower courts, the decision can be appealed. As the literature reviewed above indicates, repeat players bring significant advantages to bear in the appellate process. It may also be the case that the appellate court remands a decision back to a lower court, exacerbating the resource commitment demanded by the litigation.

Have-Nots as Winners

As the previous pages demonstrate, significant numbers of empirical studies find support for Galanter's party capability theory. Studies of both the formal legal system as well as alternatives to it find evidence that the haves typically prevail over the have-nots and that the resources attributed to repeat players appear to systematically advantage them in interactions with one-shotters. However, there may be aspects of the legal system that could offset the power patterns repeat players enjoy. More liberal judges may tend to support individual plaintiffs, and juries can serve a redistributive role favoring the have-nots over the haves (Robbennolt 2002). There are some studies that do not support Galanter's thesis, or at least do not find the pervasive advantage Galanter seems to suggest. These studies do not so much undermine Galanter's theoretical premise as they uncover the resources that one-shotters can secure to counterbalance the systemic advantages of the haves.

Galanter concedes that there are counterbalances to the power of the repeat players. Among these resources are skilled legal representatives and interest groups whom one-shotters can attract for a variety of reasons to their case. In addition, the ideological preferences of judges and juries can offset the disadvantages the have-nots face in the adjudicative process.

Under a mechanistic perception of the law, the attorney simply facilitates the application of the appropriate rule—that is, the law—to the facts presented by the client before her. The outcome for any individual plaintiff will be positive when the law clearly favors the plaintiff, and less so otherwise. However, the "indeterminacy" of the law, as Wilkins (1990) characterizes it, or its malleability, as the legal realists argue, provides a great deal of leverage for articulate and knowledgeable attorneys. Understanding the rules allows for procedural maneuvers that benefit a client. Past interactions with court personnel, both personal and professional, can benefit an individual. Access to skilled legal researchers who can craft legal arguments from the myriad of precedents available may prove persuasive to particular judges or juries. Significant financial resources can fund delays, obfuscation, and investigations, which may eliminate the ability of the opposition to continue. Indeed, Wilkins argues that "a system in which some clients can buy their way out of legal limitations exemplifies the kind of power-driven regime that the rule of law is supposed to avoid" (495–96). While scholars debate the ethical line between appropriate advocacy and inappropriate manipulation of the system, finding and funding gifted legal talent can advance the capability of one party over another.

Lawyers as Repeat Players

As noted previously, Galanter submits that lawyers represent a special advantage for repeat players. Skilled legal advocates can potentially equalize the legal playing field, and Galanter suggests that repeat players have a greater ability to secure talented representatives. Moreover, repeat players are more likely to have long-term relationships with attorneys, who are unlikely to risk ongoing partnerships for a significant personal gain in any one case. Attorneys will evaluate for the long haul and litigate accordingly. Attorneys for one-shotters have no such concerns. Their litigation decisions are decided seriatim and are more likely to represent the attorney's long-term professional concerns than the client's. Effective counsel may also be able to accurately pick winners and settle losers (Harris, Peeples, and Metzloff 2005, 2008).

At the time of Galanter's study, the legal services movement viewed the mobilization of the law as a key mechanism to facilitate courts as change agents (Grossman, Kritzer, and Macaulay 1999; Kritzer 2003; Lempert 1976). The federal Legal Services Program was founded to empower individuals fighting for social and economic rights. Poverty lawyers were seen as a catalyst for expanding access to courts, challenging governmental power, and developing substantive and procedural rights for the poor (Harris 2003). Galanter agrees that public interest law firms can serve as surrogate repeat players for one-shotters. If one-shotters are able to gain access to capable attorneys, either through structural mechanisms such as contingency fee arrangements or through legal services programs, can such an advantage create a repeat player out of a one-shotter?

Scholars have expended significant effort evaluating the role of lawyers in litigation outcomes. Miller and Sarat (1980–81) conducted a survey of households in five federal judicial districts in 1980 to determine the occurrence of civil disputes in the general population, focusing on the number who experienced grievances, those who sought a remedy, and disagreements that resulted in a disputed claim. According to those surveyed, 68 percent of those who made a claim eventually won at least in part. However, lawyers and courts seem to play a smaller role in what the authors consider "middle-range" disputes—claims involving $1,000 or more. Fewer than 25 percent of individuals engaged in the types of middle-range disputes analyzed in the study utilized a lawyer. The primary exceptions were post-divorce and tort cases; the former essentially requires an attorney and the latter can be obtained through contingency fee arrangements.

Mather (1998) similarly finds that trial lawyers can provide a key resource for the have-nots. In evaluating tobacco litigation, she finds that only by pooling resources could the various individual plaintiffs overcome the immense imbalance of resources between the one-shotters and the repeat players. Mather's analysis of the *Cipollone v. Liggett Group, Inc.* trial in 1988 provides stark evidence of the mountain that plaintiffs must scale to defeat massive repeat players like Liggett. Liggett had decades of experience defending these types of suits. The Cipollone case alone involved more than one hundred motions, several pretrial appeals, a four-month jury trial, argument and then reargument before the Supreme Court, ultimately consuming more than $3,000,000 on the plaintiff's side (for a $400,000 jury award), but more than twenty-five times that was spent by the defense (Mather 1998, 905). However, as Cartwright (1975) predicts, winning was insufficient to overcome the resources of the repeat players. The lawyers for the Cipollone family could no longer afford to litigate the various legal claims remaining that were remanded by the Supreme Court to the district court to resolve; the attorneys abandoned the claim, and the lawsuit was dismissed.

While the Cipollone family ultimately lost, Mather argues that the victory proved critical when its symbolic effects were combined with a changing social and political antismoking climate. Cause lawyers, combined with wealthier product liability firms, developed legal strategies that ultimately secured a $368.5 billion settlement in 1997. Thus a true one-shotter such as the Cipollone family had insufficient resources to prevail, as Galanter would predict, but by tapping the expertise and financial strength of multiple law firms and the attorneys general of multiple states, the individual one-shotter claims merged into a mammoth one-shotter represented by repeat player legal talent. Critically, as Mather notes, judges could order tobacco companies to "produce documents, answer interrogatories, respond to motions, or answer objections" and "they provided a mechanism with potential to damage the industry" (Mather 1998, 936). The concern for public exposure, combined with the shifting political zeitgeist, strongly motivated tobacco companies to settle.

Kessler (1990) studies organizations that facilitate legal services that could support parties with fewer capabilities. Kessler studies five legal services programs that vary in locale (urban and rural) and in the size of the staff and the population served. Kessler finds, as Galanter argues, that professional constraints limit the ability of the lawyers associated with these agencies to pursue broader litigation and lobbying strategies that are viewed "as fundamentally inappropriate for members of the bar" (132). One of the rural attorneys practicing on behalf of the agency filed preliminary papers for a discrimination lawsuit against the major employer in the county, a coal company; the sole judge in the town subsequently prohibited the attorney from appearing before him. Such direct negative reactions are rare, but threats of negative sanctions are more common, according to Kessler, especially in rural settings. According to Kessler, the ability of the bar to serve as a tool for the have-nots was severely constrained by the practical realities of power politics.

Dumas, Haynie, and Dabavol (2015) evaluate whether or not attorneys who practice in larger firms, where presumably they have access to greater resources and expertise, prevail in civil trials. In their evaluation of more than nine hundred civil jury trials in Alabama, Indiana, Kentucky, and Tennessee, the authors find that the true resource advantage is a local one. When the plaintiff is represented by a local firm and the defendant is not, the plaintiff is more likely to win. The ability of a lawyer to navigate local legal culture can significantly benefit one-shotters over repeat players.

Harris (1999, 2003) studies the outcomes in legal disputes for the proto-typical have-nots—homeless families. Given Bezdek's (1992) rather bleak picture for tenants, one would anticipate even less success for the homeless, but the findings indicate that the purchase of legal talent can facilitate positive litigation outcomes. Harris studies right-to-home class action lawsuits filed by legal services lawyers in at least eight states. She finds that poverty lawyers are able to use favorable precedents as important symbolic resources. These decisions influence the rule-making process in the implementation phase. Lawyers provide a significant resource for the have-nots both in litigation and in securing the benefits provided to them by favorable precedents.

Lederman's (2006) study of tax court litigation finds that experienced counsel is critical to success in litigation, but not to the amount awarded for cases filed in the mid-1990s. Both the presence of an attorney and the years of the attorney's experience increase the likelihood of winning at trial and significantly reduce the tax liability of the plaintiff. However, there is no sim-ilar benefit for taxpayers in settlement awards. The finding suggests that one-shotters who can obtain a repeat player as their legal adviser will fare better at court, but one-shotters are able to hold their own absent an attorney against the government in settlement negotiations. Of course, Galanter would argue that only individuals with wealth are able to litigate, and when they do, their power to hire an experienced lawyer exacerbates their advantage in the sys-tem. Lederman's findings parallel those of Kinsey and Stalans (1999, 2003), who similarly find that the presence of an experienced attorney is an advan-tage in tax litigation.

As noted above, Bingham's study of employment discrimination finds that among one-shotters in employment arbitration hearings, white-collar execu-tives, who presumably have greater resources than pink-collar or blue-collar workers, fare better than the latter two categories in these disputes. More criti-cally for this discussion, Bingham (1997) finds that the presence of an attorney significantly increases the chance of success against employers. One-shotters who face repeat players can level the playing field by obtaining representation. Harris, Peeples, and Metzloff (2008) find that experienced attorneys are also critical to success in medical malpractice lawsuits. They studied 348 malprac-tice cases filed in North Carolina between 1992 and 1995; the winners clearly benefited from hiring attorneys with more years of experience in the profession and attorneys who had handled more cases in the past. Individuals who hire attorneys who have been practicing longer and have some experience litigating malpractice claims are more likely to succeed. This advantage is further confirmed in Ryo's (2018) study of immigration bond hearings, where represented detainees are significantly more likely to be granted bond than those without representation.

Bradt and Rave (2019) find that one-shotters can benefit substantially by pooling their claims to attract repeat player representation. Their study of multidistrict litigation (MDL), for example the opioid epidemic claims, Volkswagen diesel fraud claims, BP oil spill claims, and so on, finds that the aggregation of thousands of claims attracts an elite group of repeat player attorneys whose knowledge of MDL rules, access to capital, and economies of scale increase the probability of overall success.[5]

For criminal courts, Nardulli's (1978) study of plea agreements does not find an advantage for repeat players. In examining plea agreements in Chicago's criminal courts, Nardulli discovers that defendants represented by attorneys who are considered "regulars" before the courts fare no better than others at the preliminary hearing and actually receive longer sentences when represented by "regulars" if they plead guilty. These findings were replicated in a subsequent study of plea bargains across multiple states from 1979 to 1980 in which he found that the defendants represented by the "insider" defense bar did not fare better than those represented by outsiders (Nardulli 1986). Naradulli suggests that those attorneys who appear more regularly in the court are less likely to risk ongoing relationships with court personnel than outsiders, who are able to be more aggressive.

Unlike Nardulli, Phillips and Ekland-Olson (1982) find that defense attorneys who are repeat players before their courts do not provoke more severe sentences for their clients, but also do not produce lesser sentences. Neither the amount of contact with an attorney nor whether the attorney was court-appointed or private counsel had an effect on the sentence.

However, in appellate courts, McGuire (1995) finds that experienced lawyers increase the likelihood of success. McGuire's analysis of Supreme Court decisions from 1977 to 1982 reveals that regardless of the status of the litigants, parties represented by advocates with repeat appearances before the court are more likely to win when facing an opponent with fewer appearances. Repeat player lawyers significantly advantage their one-shot clients.

Brace and Hall (2001) argue that it is not merely the presence of an attorney with repeat experience that matters but the availability of attorneys generally. If there are greater numbers of lawyers in any given state, the ability of a one-shotter to mobilize appeals increases. They find that as the number of lawyers per 1,000 population increases, both the docket space allotted to the have-nots and the likelihood of their success increase for cases in which an amicus brief is attached. However, they find no effect for increased availability of legal skills for the remainder of the docket. Only for those cases in which the one-shotter is able to attract external attention to the case does the effect of larger numbers of attorneys in the state matter. While appeals can be more readily facilitated with access to legal talent, Boyd (2015) finds that the government and businesses are "asymmetrically advantaged" in their ability to do so (313). Litigant status differentially affects the likelihood of an appeal.

In their study of the product liability decisions of the courts of appeal from 1982 to 1993, Haire, Lindquist, and Hartley (1999) find that one-shot plaintiffs lost more frequently when represented by attorneys who lacked knowledge of the institutional characteristics of the bench before which they were advocating, especially an understanding of the political ideology of the judges who occupied that bench. In fact, they find that such "process expertise" was more critical than the attorney's knowledge of the legal principles of product liability law. Appellants lost significantly more often if their counsel had no prior experience before the circuit; however, substantive expertise did not have a significant effect. These findings suggest that understanding the culture of the court and its informal norms can benefit one-shotters who are able to retain advocates with experience before a specific court. More recent studies of the effect of lawyers as a causal mechanism before the courts of appeal find that the haves tend to prevail when securing more, more experienced, and better-educated attorneys (Haire and Moyer 2008; Szmer, Songer, and Bowie 2016).

McGuire and Caldeira (1993) find that substantive expertise has a positive effect on outcomes. Appellants represented by professional obscenity litigators have a greater likelihood of their case being selected by the US Supreme Court for review than others. Presumably, repeat player litigators have an ability to shape the legal arguments in a manner amenable to at least four of the justices. Those litigants who can hire these specialized advocates increase their chances of getting their case before the court. These results are confirmed for litigants in immigration courts, who are better off with no attorney than with a poor attorney as defined by the attorney's workload and prior success (Miller, Camp Keith, and Holmes 2015).

McAtee and McGuire (2007) find that the deference to counsel is tempered by issue salience. If justices find the case to be a particularly salient one, they are less likely to be influenced by the arguments of counsel, regardless of expertise or capability. They note that the advantage evidenced when the appellant is represented by a more experienced and more capable advocate (as measured by Justice Blackmun's ratings of lawyers who argued before the court) dissipates for salient cases. The repeat player advantage these lawyers achieve has its limitations.

Baum (1977) finds that the bar can shape outcomes in a quite different manner. His study of the Court of Patent Appeals suggests that the court was initially deferential to the administrative decisions of patent officials but that support diminished as the patent bar was able to shape the bench with patent specialists. These appointments create a bench whose policies differ from those of the generalist courts and skews more favorably to the patent bar's preferences. As Baum notes, this creates among the patent bar "a powerful incentive to influence appointments of judges" (845).

The Solicitor General

One special category of experienced counsel is the solicitor general, who serves as the government's attorney in challenges before the US Supreme Court. The solicitor general serves as a highly specialized repeat player. The solicitor general is able strategically to select those cases most likely to succeed on appeal, as well as those cases the solicitor general will support through the filing of amicus briefs. Zorn (2002) finds that the success of the solicitor general before the court depends on the initial decision to appeal. The solicitor general's expertise shapes the evaluation of the cost, the presence of factors that increase the probability of the court granting review, and the likelihood of success on the merits of the case.

Beyond the decision to appeal, a number of scholars have evaluated whether or not repeat appearances before the court benefit the litigants that the solicitor general supports. Segal and Reedy (1988) find that sex discrimination cases argued before the court from 1971 to 1984 were directly shaped by the solicitor general's position. Segal (1988) also discovers that the mere presence of a brief by the solicitor general significantly increases the likelihood of winning. The solicitor general need not participate in oral arguments to have an effect. Spriggs and Wahlbeck (1997) find that the solicitor general's repeat player status benefits litigants for whom the office files an amicus brief. The arguments of the solicitor general are more likely to be included in the court's opinion than are the arguments of other amici participants. McGuire

(1998), however, finds that the success of the office is not because the solicitor general is a special kind of repeat player, just that it is a repetitive one. That is, the success of the solicitor general's office owes primarily to the repeated appearances of counsel before the court and the benefits gained by such experience. Once that experience is controlled for, any particular deference or capability associated with the office itself is not apparent.

In a more sophisticated test of the role of the solicitor general, Baily, Kamoie, and Maltzman (2005) suggest the success is driven by greater levels of the "process expertise" articulated by Haire, Lindquist, and Hartley (1999). The solicitor general's intimate knowledge of the court and particularly of its justices provides a unique advantage in oral arguments. The solicitor general wins disproportionately (Black and Owens 2012), though the success rate varies over time, in part because of the difficulty in persuading ideological foes (see, e.g., Curry 2015). Indeed, they argue, "The 'tenth justice' is no less political than the other nine" (Bailey, Kamoi, and Maltzman 2005, 83). However, Wohlfarth (2009) argues that the office of the solicitor general has become more politicized as presidents, beginning with Reagan, have sought to advance their policy agendas through the work of the solicitor general. He finds that the solicitor general's use of amicus briefs increasingly reflects the ideology of the president. More critically, he finds that as politicization of the office increases, the likelihood of success before the Supreme Court declines. As political drivers become more critical, the repeat player expertise of the solicitor general no longer dominates decisions, lessening the likelihood of success of the solicitor general before the Supreme Court.

Interest Groups as Repeat Players

Rosenstone and Hansen (1993) suggest that mobilizing interests is indeed complicated, challenging, and "heavily weighted in favor of the advantaged" (241). Their analysis of political participation follows as "same song, second verse" to Schattschneider's (1960) and Schlozman's (1984) chorus of inequality among interest representation in American pressure groups.

Other scholars focus on the ability of these groups, once mobilized, to actually influence policy. Heinz et al. (1993) find "considerable uncertainty" in "terms of who won and who lost," as opposed to the predictable outcomes expected by Schattschneider or Schlozmanz. Smith (1984) finds that the "resource advantage" is contingent on a number of factors, including the size of the supporting coalitions.[6] However, Clawson, Neustadtl, and Scott (1992) argue that business groups' influence is "pervasive" (24). Indeed, they suggest that "businesses are enormously powerful, are not democratically run, give significant amounts of PAC money, use that money to gain access not available to other groups and advance interests different from those of the general population" (158).[7] This overwhelming advantage is achieved primarily because, contrary to pluralist theory, competing business groups do not cancel each other's interests to create an equilibrium in policy space; rather, "business is usually politically unified" (159). Corporate political action committees may have different, even competing interests on specific issues, but their power is derived from the hegemonic view of furthering profit, which leads to, if not support for one another, a lack of opposition. Others avoid conflict by concentrating on issue niches (Browne 1990). Silberman and Durden (1976) note that legislators respond to "stronger and better organized groups" (in this case labor unions) and not simply to the general bias of business groups (19; see also Kau and Rubin 1981). Quinn and Shapiro (1991) find a similarly positive effect of PAC contributions on legislative voting, but the effect was the least significant when compared to the effect of constituency, ideology, or party, and was significantly constrained by the organizational arrangements that facilitate fundraising (see also Denzau and Munger 1986).

Research seems to suggest that resources matter to the extent that organizations are dependent on them to acquire members, mobilize their participation, and gain access to policymakers. Interest groups face similar concerns in courts of law. Substantial research focuses on interest groups' use of litigation as a mechanism for shaping public policy. Scholars focus both on case sponsorship and on amicus participation. While interest groups are rarely the actual plaintiff in these cases, their participation presumably brings significant resources to bear. Galanter (1974) argues that interest groups offer an avenue for one-shotters to aggregate into repeat players, thus "upgrading" their capabilities (141–42).

However, Galanter suggests that interest groups are typically involved in litigation as a mechanism to shape the rules through "test cases." When these groups align with one-shotters, the objectives of the two can differ. As Galanter notes, "By definition, a test case—litigation deliberately designed to procure rule-change—is an unthinkable undertaking for an OS," who he argues is concerned with the "tangible outcome" of the case rather than with changing the rules for subsequent litigants (1974, 136).

Galanter (1974) also suggests that those who turn to courts as an avenue to shape public policy "tend to represent relatively isolated interests, unable to carry the day in more political forums" (135). Moreover, he views courts as passive and limited in their ability to shape rules that can be useful to the have-nots. Should a "favorably inclined court" grant a change in the rules that advantage have-nots, Galanter suggests that achieving substantive change may prove more difficult than achieving a symbolic victory in court (137–39). Thus structural and procedural constraints may limit the motivation of organizations to champion the causes of have-nots in courts of law.

The early works of Vose (1966, 1967) and Hakman (1966) led Galanter to believe that case sponsorship was a relatively rare phenomenon, as he anticipated, even at the appellate level, where its strategic use would be most likely. Subsequent scholars evaluated the use of courts by groups seeking either to protect ground gained or to expand their success in the public policy arena.

Olson (1990) asserts that certain types of policies attract the attention of interest groups more than others. Her study of civil litigation in the Minnesota federal district court finds that regulatory issues attract greater numbers of groups but that redistributive policies garner broader participation of interest groups in litigation. Olson does not see litigation as a strategy for the have-nots but as an avenue for the haves to achieve their policy goals by facilitating litigation on behalf of one-shotters.

O'Connor's (1980) study of women's groups' use of the courts finds these groups participate either as a sponsor or through amicus involvement in the majority of gender discrimination claims brought to the US Supreme Court. Her findings are in contradiction to Hakman's findings and Galanter's expectations. O'Connor and Epstein's (1981) subsequent investigation of amicus participation in the US Supreme Court from 1928 to 1980 finds that amicus curiae participation rose from 1.6 percent of cases to over 50 percent of cases by 1980. Among the cases most likely to have amicus briefs filed were those involving unions, gender or race discrimination, freedom of the press, and church-state issues. While their study does not delineate which side the organizations support, it does provide evidence that organizations, as repeat players, increasingly are recognizing courts as important avenues for shaping the rules. Indeed, the authors note that "*amicus curiae* participation by private groups is now the norm rather than the exception" (318). The critical question of "does it matter" remained unanswered.

O'Connor and Epstein (1982) attempt to answer that question in their study of interest group participation in employment disputes. They find that the success rate of cases in which interest groups are involved is approximately 58 percent for race and gender discrimination in employment cases. While this success rate by more liberal interest groups was not monolithic, it was seen as motivation by conservative groups to replicate its potential. Both O'Connor and Epstein (1983) and Epstein (1985) find increasing levels of conservative interest group involvement but less success than their more liberal counterparts (Epstein 1985). Subsequent work by Epstein and Rowland (1991) finds no significant differences in success for cases filed before the US district courts. Using an experimental design, the authors study similar types of cases, one with and one without group sponsorship. They argue that the findings "call into question the ability of groups to affect legal outcomes" (213).

Tauber (1998) also finds no benefit from amicus briefs filed on behalf of those appealing their death sentences. Scrutinizing 217 capital cases decided by the US Court of Appeals, Tauber analyzes the effect of the NAACP Legal Defense Fund as a case sponsor or amicus participant and discovers no significant effects after controlling for both legal and extralegal factors. Lindquist, Martinek, and Hettinger (2007) also find no effect for amicus participation in mixed-outcomes cases decided by the US courts of appeals.

Yarnold (1995) surveyed the 126 organizations involved in abortion cases before federal district courts from post-Roe to 1990. The results demonstrate that certain interest groups, Planned Parenthood in particular, received preferential treatment in courts. Yarnold attributes this success not merely to their repeat player status but also to their well-established reputations and to the political factors at play in abortion litigation. In particular, Yarnold suggests that the repeat player status of the ACLU and Planned Parenthood serves the groups and the pro-choice movement well. In contrast, she argues that pro-life groups were largely absent in district court abortion litigation, creating a "lopsided" affair that benefited the "play for the rules" strategy of the pro-choice organizations. The pro-life groups clearly corrected course.

Songer, Kuersten, and Kaheny (2000) find mixed effects when groups participate in litigation, but the effect varies by the status of the litigant. The authors analyze a random sample of cases filed with and without amicus briefs from 1983 through 1990 in the state supreme courts of South Carolina, Georgia, and North Carolina. The general success rate of individuals is significantly less than that of businesses or state and local governments, as Galanter would predict. However, when the results are disaggregated into those with and those without group involvement, individuals' success rates climb from 40 percent to 55 percent, higher than that for businesses with groups filing briefs on their behalf (52 percent success rate) but still somewhat lower than that of state and local governments (62 percent). In all cases, litigants' success rates climb with amicus participation, but the effect is much higher for individuals than for businesses or governments. Their results suggest that repeat players who support one-shotters in litigation can have a strong effect.

Collins (2004) analyzes amicus participation before the US Supreme Court and also finds a positive effect for litigants whose cases are championed by interest group organizations based on cases argued during the Warren and Burger courts (1953–85). The results suggest that amicus briefs marginally benefit both the petitioner and respondent after controlling for other variables. In addition, the solicitor general's support for respondents significantly advantages them. The number of participants appearing on each brief was less critical than the number of briefs filed in the case.

A study of HIV litigation by Aiken and Musheno (1994) also finds that when the claims of plaintiffs attract supporters and their resources, such as the ACLU and Lambda Legal Defense, they are more likely to succeed. Based on both focused interviews and 184 court rulings in HIV-related litigation from 1983 to 1989, the authors demonstrate that HIV-infected patients, particularly children, can have success in court when advantaged with third-party support.

Hazelton and Hinkle (2022) study the effect of amicus briefs on the decisions of the US Supreme Court. They find that attorneys matter, and more attorneys matter more. Measuring attorney impact through amicus brief participation, they find that a larger number of briefs matters, but the experience, expertise, and cooperation of the attorneys who draft the briefs affect the likelihood of the Supreme Court selecting the case, as well as the outcome and language of the final opinion.

From a party capability perspective, there is a symbiotic relationship between interest groups and litigants, especially one-shotters. One-shotters are limited by their lack of experience, knowledge, and access to resources. Interest groups as repeat players interested in shaping the rules of the legal arena need willing one-shotters (or other willing repeat players) to effect a litigation strategy. One-shotters lose control but gain the advantage of a repeat player. Interest groups gain access to the system by sponsoring or supporting one-shotters. Ultimately, the one-shotter versus repeat player interaction of the initial claim resembles more closely a repeat player versus repeat player challenge. As Olson (1990) notes, "Litigation is sufficiently expensive to require a threshold level of resources" (859). For some one-shotters, that threshold is impossible to cross absent interest group patronage.

Ideology and Repeat Player Status

Studies of judicial decision making find repeated evidence that the policy preferences of judges matter. Legal realists at the turn of the twenty-first century recognized that judges possess individual philosophies that often favor one perspective over another, regardless of the facts and the law (Cohen 1914; Frank 1930; Llewellyn 1931; Pound 1910). Cardozo (1921) perhaps articulates this perspective best when he argues that "there is in each of us a stream of tendency, whether you choose to call it philosophy or not, which gives coherence and direction to thought and action. . . . We may try to see things as objectively as we please. None the less, we can never see them with any eyes except our own" (12–13).

Pritchett's (1948) early work on the US Supreme Court identified blocks of judges who appeared to share similar judicial philosophies, as evidenced by voting patterns across particular issue areas. Schubert's (1965, 1974) work later characterized these policy preferences as representing the justices' ideologies. Segal and Spaeth (1996b) are best known for their work identifying judges as pursuing their policy preferences in their votes. Using quantitative measures of judicial ideology, Segal and Cover (1989) analyze the voting patterns of Supreme Court justices and find remarkably stable voting patterns that align with the justices' ideologies. While subsequent work consistently finds that ideology matters, research also finds that the decision calculus is more complex than judges simply voting only for their preferred policy outcome in the case.

The bulk of the research studying the effect of ideology on judicial decision-making focuses primarily on the US Supreme Court. Research has examined its effect on agenda setting (Boucher and Segal 1995; Krohl and Brenner 1990; Palmer 1982; Perry 1991; Ulmer 1984), on deference to stare decisis (Brenner and Stier 1996; Brisbin 1996; Knight and Epstein 1996; Segal and Spaeth 1996a, 1999; Songer and Lindquist 1996; Spriggs and Hansford 2001), and on the interaction with case facts (George and Epstein 1992; Segal 1984). Similar efforts have examined the effects of ideology on the US courts of appeals (Haire, Lindquist, and Hartley 1999; Lindquist, Martinek, and Hettinger 2007; Songer 2000; Songer, Sheehan, and Haire 1999, 2003) and for state supreme courts (Brace and Hall 1990, 1993, 1997; Hall 1987; Songer, Kuersten, and Kaheny 2000). These citations are by no means exhaustive but merely representative of the extensive empirical work examining appellate decision-making in US courts.

Galanter's thesis focuses primarily on trial courts, where there has been less work on the effects of ideology. Ashenfelter, Eisenberg, and Schwab (1995) study federal trial courts and find that ideology has no effect on the "mass of case outcomes" (257). The authors study federal civil rights and prisoner cases filed in two US federal district courts, some 2,250 cases, in 1981. Their results suggest that neither party affiliation nor party of the appointing president affects the outcomes in the cases, at least the decisions of judges involved in the randomly assigned cases they studied.

Carp and Rowland (1983) find the effect of the appointing president at the federal trial-court level is less than at the appellate level, but still significant. Rowland, Songer, and Carp (1988), however, find "unprecedented" polarization between judges appointed by President Reagan and those appointed by President Carter, paralleling the earlier work of Rowland, Carp, and Stidham (1984), which finds substantial differences in support for criminal defendants among federal district court judges. Judges appointed by President Johnson were more supportive of criminal defendants than were judges appointed by President Kennedy. Those appointed by President Nixon were the least supportive of criminal defendants' claims.

Recognizing the critical role of the home state senators' preferences in the appointment of federal judges, Johnson and Songer (2002) compare the influence of the appointing president's preferences and that of the home state senator in federal district court judges' voting patterns. In their examination of civil liberties, economic and labor, and criminal procedure cases decided between 1961 and 1995, the authors find that the political preferences of the appointing president were the dominating force.

Studies of the effect of ideology at the state trial courts are rare. A number of sentencing studies of state trial courts examine such variables as race and gender (see, e.g., Daly and Tonry 1997; Spohn, Gruhl, and Welch 1981–82; Unnever, Frazier, and Henretta 1980), but the inclusion of judicial ideology in the analysis is less common. Pruitt and Wilson (1983) include the ideology of the judge in their predictors of sentences for armed robbery and burglary defendants in Milwaukee's criminal courts from 1967 to 1977. They find that more liberal judges assigned significantly lower sentences than their more conservative counterparts, at least in the earlier periods of their study. They find no effect by the later years.

Dumas and Haynie's (2012) study of civil trial courts finds no evidence of judicial ideology affecting outcomes. While judges are typically directly involved in criminal sentencing, they are less so in civil trials. Dumas and

Haynie speculate that judges could serve as a filter for evidence presented at trial and thus have some influence on the framing of information provided to the jury, indirectly affecting jury decisions. The results present no evidence of judges' ideology affecting the likelihood of a pro-plaintiff verdict or the award amount should the plaintiff prevail.

While Galanter's thesis focuses on the advantages of the haves primarily in trial courts, he does recognize the importance of appeals for repeat players who play for the rules given the potentially pervasive effect of appellate court decisions. Galanter does not address specifically the role of ideology in repeat player versus one-shotter interactions, but inevitably, its presence could potentially temper the advantage of the "haves." Conversely, the potential of an appellate loss may exacerbate the risk-averse behavior of repeat players, leading to even greater likelihood of winning at the appellate level. That is, repeat players may be even more discerning in their selection of cases, appealing only those for which they have greater confidence in their ability to win. Moreover, some level of resources is required to pursue appeals, suggesting that the advantages enjoyed at trial, or especially pre-trial, may persist at the appellate level. However, one-shotters may have some advantages at the appellate level. As the previous research demonstrates, experienced litigators prove especially critical in the US Supreme Court. It may also be the case that one-shotters who might otherwise abandon their losses are capable of appeals because of interest group sponsorship. The commitment of one-shotters to pursue their goals may prevent settlement if the power of organized interests is behind them. Despite the risk-averse behavior Galanter assigns to repeat players, they can be forced to litigate.

Manning and Randazzo (2009) find there are issue areas where appeal courts appear to protect weaker parties. Their analysis of health care policy cases before the US courts of appeals finds that individuals enjoy an advantage over any level of the government. In the most comprehensive study of haves and have-nots before the US Supreme Court, Sheehan, Mishler, and Songer (1992) find that the ideology of the court affects the likelihood of a particular litigant category winning in their study of decisions from 1953 to 1988. Individuals as appellants had a much greater likelihood of success before more liberal courts than did businesses. The authors argue that "litigant success before the Supreme Court depends substantially on the ideological composition of the Court, but little if at all, on the resources and prior judicial experience of the litigants" (470). Other work also finds that ideology has a significant effect but finds that the resources of the federal government overpower almost every other advantage foes bring to bear when challenged by or challenging them in court. That brings us to a special category of repeat player, the government.

Government as Gorilla

Shapiro (1981) argues that the government looms exceptionally large in the legal system. The government facilitates the establishment of both constitutional and statutory law, and while courts, and the judges who staff them, are theoretically to be both independent and impartial, Shapiro argues the ideal is incompatible with the reality of the institutionalization of legal systems. He contends that prior to the development of formalized adjudicative bodies, individuals or organizations in conflict agree to settle their differences, that is, they "consent" to a solution or to a procedure to reach an agreement. Once the formal legal structure is in place, "consent" is replaced with the coercive nature of the law. Individuals are compelled to participate in civil litigation or are brought to court for violating social norms enumerated in criminal statutes. The prototypical court, Shapiro argues, is one that involves an independent judge who applies preexisting legal norms after adversary proceedings to determine who is assigned legal fault—the loser—and who is not—the winner (1). The triad of conflict resolution pits the government against a plaintiff or defendant before a judicial arbiter. Shapiro maintains that rather than an adversarial conflict in which the two battle before a neutral umpire, the triad devolves into two against one, given that the judiciary itself is the government.

Shapiro argues that "the notion of an 'independent judiciary,' which is central to the conventional prototype of courts, is simply an elaborate rationalization for the substitution of coercion for consent. The state now imposes a judge on the parties. The judge is openly and admittedly a state official. It is repeatedly asserted, nonetheless, that the judge is 'independent.' The myth of judicial independence is designed to mollify the loser" (65).

Shapiro suggests that the government's heavy hand is pervasive in the rules that govern the conflicts. More critically, he argues, the government employs the very individuals tasked to determine the winners and losers. Despite their best efforts, the nature of the government's ability to staff the legal system from stem to stern inevitably leads to judges engaging in politics. As Shapiro notes, "Like most other political institutions, courts tend to be loaded with multiple political functions, ranging under various circumstances from bolstering the legitimacy of the political regime to allocating scarce economic resources or setting major social policies" (63).

Shapiro's thesis presents the foundational structure for Galanter's argument that the government is "a special kind of RP" (Galanter 1974, 111). Galanter shares Shapiro's perspective that the coercive nature of the government limits the strategic choices of one-shotters and even repeat players. For example, Galanter argues that repeat players can use the threat of severing business relationships with other repeat players to facilitate resolutions. Repeat players are not able, however, to withdraw from relationships with government entities given the obligatory interactions required to persist in the marketplace. Government regulations demand ongoing associations (111–12). As Galanter notes, "Withdrawal of future association is not possible in dealing with the government" (112). Thus Galanter expects "litigation by and against government to be more frequent than in other RP versus RP situations" (112). What Galanter does not address is whether the government as a "special" repeat player is more likely to win. To the extent that the government theoretically has unlimited resources, Galanter's thesis would predict it to have a greater likelihood of success. Like Shapiro, he also recognizes that the rules are shaped by the government. Shapiro would argue that those rules will over time benefit the government, and the decisions of the courts will as well.[8]

Substantial empirical evidence supports the proposition that the government is acutely advantaged and enjoys greater success as a result. Kritzer (2003) points to two specific components that drive the government's advantage. The first is that the government makes the rules that courts enforce, and presumably the government will structure the game to its benefit. Second, he echoes Shapiro's charge that courts are agencies of the state, and despite the norm of judicial independence that judges may embrace, courts cannot be independent of the government when they are the government. From his evaluation of the empirical evidence, Kritzer concludes that "ultimately, judges are part of the regime, and when the regime comes under challenge, the government will tend to receive any breaks or benefits at the margin that might accrue" (362). The government, as he notes, presents a formidable adversary who appears to enjoy "a fundamental advantage that flows from the fact that it sets the rules by which cases are brought and decisions are made, and it is government officials, judges, who make the decisions" (361). The government also possesses "extensive structures for filtering out cases where its position is weak" (351).

Studies of litigation outcomes in criminal cases suggest that the government is especially advantaged. Meeker (1984) studies state courts of last resort from 1870 to 1970. Meeker assesses the "popular impression" at the time that "liberal appellate judges" were "freeing criminal defendants on the basis of technical loopholes" (553). Using data collected from the forty-eight contiguous states in five-year intervals, Meeker discovers that criminal defendants were more likely to lose except in the late 1800s. While the Northeast provides some contrast to the rest of the country, the odds of winning a criminal appeal declined from 1870 to 1925 and then began to increase until the 1960s and 1970s.

Davies (1982) also studies the myth of the "imperial judiciary." In an analysis of the criminal appeals in a California Intermediate Appellate Court, Davies finds that only 4.8 percent of 544 criminal appeals reviewed in 1974 were reversed, though the court altered the decision of the lower court in a larger, but still small, percentage of cases—14 percent. By either metric, the government enjoyed a significant advantage.

At the trial court level, the advantage of the government is even stronger. For the 75,573 criminal cases disposed of by the federal district courts in 2002, 95 percent were disposed of through a guilty plea (Pastore and Maguire 2003). Not only does the prosecutor have structural advantages in the plea negotiation, but the initial indictment procedures overwhelmingly favor the prosecutor; the defendant is not even a party to the proceedings (Albonetti 1987; Ball 2006). Moreover, research demonstrates that defendants who press for the right to trial are more likely to be sentenced to prison (Dixon 1995) and receive harsher sentences (Dixon 1995; Steffensmeier and Demuth 2000; Steffensmeier and Hebert 1999) than those who do not, incentivizing further the decision to plea. Ulmer and Bradley's (2006) study of criminal sentencing data in Pennsylvania from 1997 to 2000 reveals that "defendants are substantially penalized if they exercise a right to a jury trial and then lose" (631). Ulmer, Eisenstein, and Johnson (2010) then investigate the argument that the "trial penalty" is largely the result of reductions for those who assist law enforcement or accept responsibility as opposed to those who do not or who obstruct law enforcement. Even after controlling for such "guidelines-based" factors, the authors find "meaningful trial penalties" (560). Galanter argues that criminal defendants typically lack the resources to combat the government, and the empirical results appear to support this at both the trial and appellate level.

In civil litigation the government also fares well. For federal trial courts, the research finds that the government prevails. Walker and Barrow (1985) examine the effect of diversity on judges' decisions in federal district courts and find race and gender do affect voting patterns. Women judges are more likely to support the government in federal economics regulation (73 percent of cases studied) compared to men (53 percent of cases), and Black judges are more likely than white judges to support the government in economic regulation litigation (62 percent to 55 percent). Regardless of race or gender, the findings support greater government success in federal district courts when the government's regulation of the economy is challenged.

Ringquist and Emmert's (1999) evaluation of federal district court rulings in environmental litigation from 1974 to 1991 discovers that government actors receive smaller penalties than do Fortune 500 companies. Eisenberg and Farber (2003) find a greater likelihood of success for the government when it is the plaintiff in job discrimination cases against private parties in federal civil trials. The authors attribute the success in part to the Equal Employment Opportunity Commission's ability to selectively sift through thousands of complaints and choose those most ripe for success.

In an analysis of over 9,000 jury awards in Cook County, Illinois, from 1959 to 1979, the results reveal that the government paid higher awards than corporations and corporations paid higher awards than individuals. However, corporations fared worse than any other litigant when the injuries were severe. Among one-shotters, Black plaintiffs lost more often and were awarded smaller amounts than white litigants (Chin and Peterson 1985). In the context of Cook County, the deep pockets of the government appear to work against it.

On the other hand, Dumas and Haynie (2012) find that individuals were more likely to prevail against corporations than against the state government in civil trials in Alabama from 2002 to 2008. Individuals also received smaller awards if successful when they faced the government as opposed to a corporation or another individual. Thus, in either federal or state trial courts in the US, studies find a government advantage, at least in some periods and for some issue areas.

Appellate courts would appear to provide the greatest potential for government success. Both Shapiro (1981) and Kritzer (2003) argue that government's ability to formulate the rules and appoint the arbiters should benefit its prospects for success. In addition, as Kritzer notes, the government can settle those cases it is likely to lose, or at least elect not to pursue appellate review if it anticipates an unfavorable judicial ruling. A number of studies appear to confirm this perspective.

Farole's (1999) study of state supreme court decisions across five states from 1975 to 1990 finds that the government tends to have greater success. Farole's analysis of almost 2,000 opinions of the supreme courts of Alabama, Kansas, New Jersey, South Dakota, and West Virginia from 1975 to 1990 in five-year increments discovers that local governments have an overall success rate as appellant and respondent of almost 57 percent, while the state fares even better, with an overall success rate of 65 percent. Both state and local governments have higher overall success rates than either businesses (49 percent), groups (46 percent), or individuals (43 percent). Criminal defendants have the lowest overall success rate, 35 percent. These results support Shapiro's argument: state courts seem to be supportive of their regimes. In Farole's analysis the government fares substantially better than any other party, and substantially better than the success rates of state supreme courts uncovered by Wheeler et al. (1987). Given that the authors study a much longer time frame, 1870 to 1970, it may be that the repeat player advantage shifts over time. Earlier studies examined in this review also suggest that longitudinal effects should not be ignored (McIntosh 1980–81; Meeker 1984; Wheeler et al. 1987).

Emmert's (1991) analysis of state supreme courts' decisions involving judicial review from 1981 to 1985 finds that criminal defendants challenge laws more frequently than other types of parties, especially defendants on death row or serving lengthy prison sentences. These parties also have the least likelihood of success, winning their appeals only 8 percent of the time. The government has the greatest success rate, winning over one-third of its challenges. Interestingly, political groups have the second highest rate of return on their investment in legal challenges, prevailing in one of every two appeals. Individuals win 24 percent of the time, and businesses fare better than criminal defendants but worse than the government, political groups, or individuals. Emmert confirms the general dominance of the government before its high court but does not find that business repeat players prevail as predicted.

Beavers and Emmert's (2000) analysis of state supreme court decisions covers a narrower time frame that falls within Farole's window of analysis and involves a smaller subset of a court's docket (those cases that involve the use of judicial review), but includes all of the states' high courts. Judicial review of state actions and statutes represents a specific instance of litigants playing for the rules. These challenges can change the structure, power, and process of politics. These challenges also represent identifiable tests of the regime's authority, which, according to Shapiro, should have a greater likelihood of success if courts are independent of the state. Beavers and Emmert find that judges in state high courts are significantly more likely to decide the appeal based on state law rather than on rationales grounded in federal law, and that this is especially true when the state government is involved. The authors assert that states prefer decisions to be based on state law because the decisions can then be altered or overturned by statute or even revisions of the state constitution. Decisions based on federal laws or the federal Constitution constrain the state's ability to alter the court's policy. The authors argue that "this finding seems consistent with previous literature that governmental litigants are especially successful in achieving their judicial goals" (13). It also supports Shapiro's claim that judges are deferential to their regimes.[9]

Studies of the federal courts of appeals have found a fairly consistent advantage for the government. In their study of the US courts of appeal, Songer and Sheehan (1992) find success heavily weighted toward the government. Their analysis of all judicial actions in 1986 for three circuits (4,281 cases) discovers that the government fares dramatically better than businesses, and businesses succeed far more often than individuals. State and local governments have an overall success rate as both plaintiff and respondent of nearly 86 percent, while the federal government is almost identical in its overall success rate at 85 percent. Businesses fare well, with an overall success rate of 57 percent, while individuals win only 12.5 percent of the time as appellant and 30.7 percent of the time as respondent. After controlling for the effects of partisan ideology, appellant status, issue type, diversity of jurisdiction cases, and region, the probability of a state government succeeding was over 80 percent in published decisions and 98 percent in unpublished opinions. The probability of the federal government succeeding in published opinions was 87 percent and 99 percent in unpublished opinions. The results provide substantial confirmation of Galanter's expectations for repeat players and one-shotters in courts of law. The authors conclude that "the haves come out ahead in the courts of appeals to an impressive degree" (254).

While Songer and Sheehan's findings are striking validation of Galanter's thesis, they represent but a single point in time. Subsequent analysis of a substantially longer period on the courts of appeal (1925–88), however, also finds that the government has greater success rates than other litigants (Songer, Sheehan, and Haire 1999). Over the entire sixty-four-year period, businesses succeeded at slightly higher rates than individuals (approximately 50 percent for the former and 40 percent for the latter), but the government continued to win a "commanding majority" of the time (over 68 percent) (827). Further, the authors find that even major shifts in the political parties of the judges composing the bench do not disturb this underlying pattern, nor does the pattern shift substantially over time.

Studies of the US Supreme Court, however, suggest that the power of the haves may not be monolithic. Early analyses of parties before the court find that the federal government, and especially federal government agencies, has particularly high success rates. Canon and Giles (1972) study appearances before the court by six government agencies for the 1957 to 1968 terms. The success rates of federal agencies range from 91 percent for the Federal Power Commission and the Federal Trade Commission to a low of 56 percent for the Immigration and Naturalization Service (INS). At worst, these agencies fare better than a flip of the coin, and at best they have only a one in ten chance of losing. Canon and Giles do find some variation by judicial ideology, with more liberal justices providing less support.

Crowley (1987) similarly examines Supreme Court review of federal agencies, focusing on those responsible for "economic" regulation, such as the Federal Energy Regulatory Commission, the Securities and Exchange Commission, and the Interstate Commerce Commission, and on "social" regulation agencies, such as the Equal Employment Opportunity Commission, the National Labor Relations Board, and the Environmental Protection Agency, to compare the success rates of the one group to the other. Economic agencies fared better before the court, winning 79 percent of the time, compared to 68 percent success rates for social agencies. He finds little variance across the two time periods studied (1976–80 and 1981–83), though the support varied significantly from conservative to liberal justices, with the former supporting economic agencies more and the latter favoring social agencies.

Sheehan (1990) reexamines Crowley's analysis of agency type before the Warren, Burger, and Rehnquist courts. He notes that economic agencies and social agencies had remarkably similar success rates before the Warren and Burger courts (between 72 percent and 76 percent) but that social agencies fared less well under Rehnquist than did economic agencies, which has a perfect win record in the seven cases heard by the Rehnquist court judges. In further analysis of the ideological direction of the decisions of the court, Sheehan does find that "justices located at the ends of the ideological spectrum were more likely to support an agency when the policy position of the agency was commensurate with their policy values" (883).

Ulmer (1985) studies the success of state and federal government litigants in civil liberties cases before the court from 1903 to 1968. The results suggest that resources play a less significant role before the apex court. Additionally, the success rates of both the federal and state governments declined over time. The federal government won 69 percent of its cases under the Fuller court, but this rate had declined to slightly under 42 percent by the end of the Warren court. The weakening of the repeat player advantage of states before the apex court is even more dramatic, falling from almost 97 percent success rates under the Fuller court to less than a one in four chance before the Warren court.

This trend clearly reverses over the next several decades. In their study of decisions before the Warren, Burger, and Rehnquist courts, Kearney and Sheehan (1992) find that state and local governments enjoyed both greater access and greater success in the post-Warren years. Their success was especially prominent in criminal procedure and civil rights cases. They attribute the government's advantage to the increasingly conservative ideology of the court from 1953 to 1989, which resulted in more conservative decisions favoring state and federal governments. As the authors note, ideology is "the single most important factor determining outcomes for or against" state and local governments (1021).

Ideology is confirmed as an important factor in litigation outcomes before the US Supreme Court in a study by Sheehan, Mishler, and Songer (1992). Analyzing the differential success rates of various litigants before the court, the authors find that the federal government has the largest advantage before the court when compared to individuals, businesses, or corporations. Compared to other legal venues, "litigant resources and experience are considerably less important" in the Supreme Court (469). The ideology of the justices diminishes the advantages that resources bring to bear for businesses, individuals, and state governments. To the extent that the authors locate any advantage for parties with presumed greater resources, the advantage "stems almost entirely from the observed dominance of the federal government," which succeeds at greater rates than any other litigant category (469).

Comparing the success before the US Supreme Court of different levels of government litigants (federal, state, and local), Myers and Downey (2017) confirm that the national government prevails over subnational governments. The national government, however, does not enjoy a similar advantage when challenging local governments.[10]

Resources, Litigants, and Outcomes

Our extensive review of the literature in general finds support for Galanter's proposition that resources matter. While the advantages enjoyed by repeat

players over one-shotters can vary depending on time, issues, judicial preferences, legal talent, external support, and so forth, the research suggests that
in the US, there is demonstrable empirical evidence that the haves do indeed
come out ahead. We now turn to studies that evaluate Galanter's thesis in
other nation-states to determine its generalizability.

2 | Party Capability Theory in a Comparative Context

AS THE PREVIOUS chapter indicates, many scholars have empirically tested Galanter's party capability theory in the US. As is clear from the empirical analyses discussed in the previous chapter, there is significant support for Galanter's overall assertion that the haves tend to prevail, at least in the context of the American legal system. Do the outcomes vary according to political, economic, and legal contexts, or is Rousseau correct in his assertion that the dominance of the strong over the weak is without exception? If Galanter's thesis is generalizable beyond the American context, we should find similar evidence of more capable parties succeeding in other countries. In this chapter we again focus on research that confirms the advantage of repeat players, the circumstances under which the have-nots might prevail, and the advantages that lawyers provide. We also review research assessing advantages that accrue to a special category of repeat player, the government.

Advantage Repeat Players

One of the earliest empirical studies that informs our knowledge of the haves versus have-nots debate outside the US was Silliman's study of the Philippine Court of Agrarian Relations (CAR) (Silliman1981–82).[1] The CAR was created in the 1950s and largely resolved landlord-tenant disputes between landowners and tenant farmers. Silliman (1981–82) studied a sample of the decisions of the CAR from 1968 to 1976 and found that despite the agrarian reform efforts that mobilized to create the CAR, it had not functioned as a "significant instrument for social change" (107). In fact, Silliman found that the CAR "operates to protect the current arrangement of wealth and social status," in part because it has neither the staff nor the resources to handle the volume of actual and potential litigation. Moreover, none of the cases in Silliman's analysis involved major exchanges of resources. Decisions may affect the distribution of resources on the margins, but the court is not an agent for significant change.

Silliman argues that despite the creation of the CAR, the rules themselves reflect a "conservative orientation" that restricts the types of issues brought before the bench. The few minor conflicts brought to the court change little of the fundamental advantages of the repeat players over the one-shotters. As a result, Silliman argues, "the evidence from Philippine agrarian law provides greater support for the view that the law is imposed from above with the aim of bolstering the dominant status of society's elite" (109).

Enhancing the ability of one-shotters to mobilize the law could restrict the capacity of repeat players to prevail. Blankenburg (1981–82, 1994) studies one such potential institution in his analysis of legal insurance in West Germany. Seen as an avenue to "remove social inequalities of access to law" (1981–82, 601), legal insurance provides coverage for lawyers' fees and court costs for individuals or corporations that want to protect themselves from the risks associated with legal conflict. Judges, on the other hand, claim that such insurance plans are responsible for increasing litigation rates. The author finds that legal insurance plans are utilized most often when the outcome of a case is less predictable and the relationships are anonymous, especially in cases of traffic accidents involving questions of liability. In these interactions the one-shot plaintiff faces a one-shot defendant who is represented by a repeat player automobile insurance company. When the plaintiff used legal insurance, the rate of success was only 19 percent in those cases that reached a final court judgment. Employee plaintiffs litigating contract issues also fared poorly (13 percent). Both mobilization and success remained highly correlated with existing inequalities.

McKie and Reed (1981) survey Canadian civil court records from 1974 and 1975 and the Central Divorce Registry of Canada from 1969 to 1977. The former provides a general picture of the state of civil litigation in Canada while the latter provides a focus for the primary legal issue encountered by women. The results demonstrate the dominance of organizations (65 percent of plaintiffs) and men (28 percent of plaintiffs) compared to women (12 percent of plaintiffs). In terms of docket space, repeat players are clearly dominant, and women, presumed to have fewer resources than men, particularly in the 1970s, mobilized the law less frequently than other litigants. Here too, McKie and Reed find that women accessed courts most frequently in traffic injuries, where women represented 36 percent of plaintiffs. In divorce proceedings, men and women were evenly split as petitioners. In sum, organizations were seen to dominate civil litigation in trial courts in Canada with the obvious exception of divorce cases, where organizations play no role. Here, women do have a more prominent role, but the inability to abrogate a marriage absent court intervention certainly skews the results. Overall, the authors find that women "*seem* to fare relatively poorly" (503).[2]

Studies of Chinese litigation outcomes parallel the findings for common law courts. He and Su (2013) study more than 2,700 civil cases from 2004 to 2009 in the courts of Shangai, "the industrial, financial, and commercial hub of China" (126). They argue that structural aspects of the Chinese legal system exacerbate the advantages of repeat players. First, the authors suggest that the way in which judges are selected limits their independence. Judges are appointed by local officials, and their subsequent career trajectory is controlled by these bureaucrats, creating an accountability to the officials rather than adherence to the rules. In addition, the courts are not immune from corruption, and relatedly, the judiciary is only now exhibiting a growing professionalism. Only recently have judges been required to have a bar qualification; the lack of formal legal and ethics training results in greater influence from extralegal forces. The accountability to elites, the potential for corruption, and the influence of extralegal factors advantage those with greater resources, who can better capitalize on all three structural weaknesses. Their findings appear to support these assertions. When a one-shotter faced a repeat player, the success rate was less than 20 percent, though one-shotters did garner at least a partial win in 32 percent of cases. Conversely, when repeat players challenged one-shotters in the Shanghai courts, they won decidedly in 43 percent of cases and won partial victories in another 40 percent. When analyzing whether legal representation ameliorates the repeat player advantage, He and Su discover that very little changes. Stronger parties win and do so by significant margins, and even after controlling for whether or not the parties enjoy legal representation, "these winning gaps remain significant and sizable" (138). The authors suggest that these courts persist in a political context that values economic development, and that judges' decisions will inevitably reflect that, especially when judges function in systems in which the rule of law is weak.[3]

Lu, Pan, and Zhang (2015) present an interesting aspect of the Chinese system in their study of 3,323 commercial lawsuits and the advantage of state-owned firms as extensions of the government. They confirm that both state-owned firms and private firms are advantaged in the legal system. This advantage is exacerbated when either has political ties to the regime and is limited when the litigation occurs in regions with stronger legal institutions. Interestingly, the authors do find that firms with local connections enjoy a home court advantage, but this advantage dissipates when the case is tried outside the home province.

Ipsen (2020) finds that corporations are able to leverage their knowledge of the local legal community in which their business is embedded. Companies may opt to litigate to shape the "rules" rather than to facilitate statutory change. Her study of the legal strategies of a large Chilean firm confirms its use of "strategic legalism."[4]

Litigants of higher socioeconomic status are also found to be advantaged in Lundholm's (2021) study of foreclosure cases in Sweden from 2000 to 2014. Lundholm argues mortgage lenders are the prototypical repeat player who are interacting with one-shot mortgage borrowers. Lundholm is interested in when the repeat player lenders foreclose on borrowers and finds that those with greater resources have greater potential for compensation compared to lower socioeconomic strata borrowers.

There are structural weaknesses that could advantage the haves as well. Kidder and Miyazawa (1993) study environmental litigation in the Japanese context, where, they argue, public conflict is disdained. Moreover, the delays and obstacles that typify legal conflicts serve as a deterrent to many potential plaintiffs, but particularly to repeat players. Plaintiffs have successfully engaged the legal system by exploiting economies of scale. In the single lawsuit studied, large numbers of lawyers (more than two hundred), who divide the labor, are able to mobilize large numbers of plaintiffs (more than five hundred), who divide the cost. This pattern has "become part of a strategy for organizing and expressing opposition to the dominant political and economic tendencies of the postwar years" (624). The ability of the one-shotter to prevail against the industries allegedly polluting is not yet known, insofar as a single case can take over a decade to reach a final verdict. Such delays benefit repeat players, who have greater resources to fund their patience.[5] The litigation strategy analyzed by Kidder and Miyazawa suggests at least one avenue for one-shotters to successfully mobilize their challenge.

More recent studies of the British appellate courts find the haves experiencing advantages, but to varying degrees. Hanretty's (2014) analysis of the decisions of the Judicial Committee of the Privy Council and the Appellate Committee of the House of Lords from 1969 to 2003 suggests that while the government does enjoy an advantage over other litigants, businesses do not appear to have any advantage. Hanretty's (2020) subsequent analysis of the UK Supreme Court confirmed that in the British context, resources can affect outcomes. The relative number of Queen's Counsel representing litigants

increased the likelihood of success, but the government advantage was evident in some issue areas (public law and chancery cases, for example) but
not in others.

Have-Nots as Winners

In other contexts, where the rule of law is weak, judges may elect to favor
those with less, appreciating the inherent inequality that drives these systems.
In interviews with justices of the Philippine Supreme Court, Tate and Haynie
(1994) find that the justices are both aware of and sensitive to the resource
differentials of litigants before them. At least some of the justices believed
it was their role to "protect the down-trodden" (220). The court, one justice
noted, subscribes to "the doctrine that he who has less in life should be more
favored in the law." Though the justice was quick to note that this does not
mean the court will openly or consistently side with the disadvantaged; the
justice recognized that "they need our protection because they are always at
a disadvantage the moment they report a case" (220). In particular, a justice
noted that in employment cases, the court has been quite sympathetic to
individual claimants, pointing to a decision in which the court rewarded an
employee terminated after eighteen years of service, because "that has been
the thinking of the Court, an obligation of some of the tenets of social justice, so that this fellow does not get thrown out in the streets after 18 years"
(220). These perspectives, however, may be constrained to the justices interviewed, though many served for decades, some both during and after the
Marcos regime.

Haynie (1994) studies the decisions of the Philippine Supreme Court from
1961 to 1986, a period coinciding with the rise and demise of the Marcos dictatorship. Her analysis finds less support for Galanter's thesis in at least some
issue areas, and the results mirror the sympathies of the justices as reflected
in the interviews. Replicating Atkins's (1991) analysis of the success of various
litigant interactions before the English Court of Appeal, Haynie finds that
individuals are more likely to win if challenging the government or a corporation. Corporations have no significant advantage when challenging individuals but fare poorly when facing the government. Governments have no
advantage when challenging individuals. Unlike Atkins, Haynie finds that the
legal underdog is more likely to win. She attributes the findings to the pro-
underdog ideologies of the justices as articulated by them in the interviews
and to particular issues. Individuals succeeded in 84 percent of the workers'

compensation challenges brought before the court but also had success in labor cases, wining 53 percent of them. In line with Galanter's expectations, corporations had greater success in economics cases, winning creditor-debtor issues 62 percent of the time and landlord-tenant issues almost 80 percent of the time. The government also succeeded in tort cases (70 percent success rate), while corporations did not (43 percent success rate). Overall, Haynie's analysis provides only mixed support for Galanter's thesis.

Haynie argues that political context may affect litigation outcomes differently. The concern for stability and legitimacy in developing economies may actually advantage one-shotters in authoritarian regimes. Haynie contends, "To enhance the stability of the court in society, decisions are rendered that favor those with less, and this likelihood increases as the Court's legitimacy is threatened. This does not prevent the court from deferring to the 'haves' for major political controversies, a handful of cases in any year. By balancing these interests, the court encourages the goals of stability and development in society" (1994, 769).

As noted previously, Shapiro (1981) argues that courts are an extension of the regime and cannot be truly independent of them. For courts that reside in nondemocratic regimes, this presents a potential enigma. Legal training almost universally emphasizes the importance of rules and of due process. Judges are trained to respect the rules and the rule of law. Directly confronting regimes that defy both could prove fatal; authoritarian rulers could simply replace the judges or abolish the courts. Rather than engaging in such frontal clashes, Haynie suggests that judges may choose to limit their support for unpopular or repressive regimes on the bulk of the docket while deferring in the politically charged cases. By doing so, courts can potentially serve a redistributive function, as she finds they do for certain issues in the Philippines.

Haynie (1995) subsequently tests her thesis that courts may be sensitive to those with less. She further analyzes the decisions of the Philippine Supreme Court to determine the effect of economic development on the court's decisions. She finds that the court is most likely to favor have-nots whose cases emanate from the least-developed regions in the country. Haynie submits that the advantages enjoyed by the haves may evolve over time. Perhaps there is "an evolution in the behavior of courts during social and legal development" (378). At a minimum, Haynie finds that "there is variation across and within nations" in litigation outcomes and that "variation appears to be related to social and economic development" (378).

While Haynie argues that social and economic factors may affect the ability of repeat players to prevail over one-shotters, Smyth (2000) finds that even in developed democratic countries, have-nots can succeed. Smyth evaluates the decisions of the High Court of Australia from 1948 to 1999. The analysis reveals little systematic support for Galanter's hypothesis. The federal government does enjoy an advantage before the High Court, but the success of other repeat players is less predictable.

Sheehan and Randazzo (2012) expand on Smyth's analysis for the Australian High Court in their study of the court's decisions from 1970 to 2003. They also find mixed support for Galanter's thesis. The national government does enjoy the highest overall success rate, at almost 53 percent, but individuals were just below the government, at 50.5 percent, higher than state governments, at approximately 48 percent, and much higher than private businesses, at 41 percent. Further, their analysis demonstrates that structural changes can affect litigation outcomes. Once the High Court gains control over its docket, individuals' success before the court increases.

In a study of environmental challenges decided by the Supreme Court of India between 1980 and 2010, Sahu (2014) finds that underdogs prevail. Sahu attributes the success of underdogs challenging both government and industry to the activist role of the Indian Supreme Court following Prime Minister Gandhi's exercise of emergency powers. He also argues that other factors, such as the "progressive and innovative approach adopted by individual judges" (55), the increasing use of public interest litigation by lawyers and activists, and efforts to strengthen statutory and administrative action that protects the environment, contributed to the have-nots prevailing more than Galanter would predict.

Dotan's analysis for the Israeli High Court of Justice also finds that the have-nots succeed against the haves (1999a, 1999b). By studying random samples of the court's files from 1986 to 1994, Dotan is able to analyze both pretrial settlements and the final decisions of the court. If courts are concerned for their legitimacy, one would expect the justices to be attentive to the claims of oppression at the hands of the Israeli military. Dotan finds that the court does not challenge the regime in its court rulings involving such petitions—the government lost fewer than 5 percent of the several thousand petitions decided by the court from 1986 to 1995—but analyses of cases settled prior to the court reaching a final decision suggests a much higher rate of success. Petitioners were successful in part or in full in over 50 percent of cases settled prior to the High Court's ruling (1999a). Dotan suggests that the High Court of Justice encouraged the settlement process to facilitate a restraint on government that it was unwilling to do in the formal adjudicative process.

In a subsequent analysis, Dotan (1999b) examines all petitions and settlements before the Israeli High Court of Justice, not merely those involving Palestinian petitioners. Dotan argues that the Israeli High Court of Justice presents an interesting laboratory in which to study repeat players versus one-shotters because the respondent is always a government agency of some sort. When the Israeli Supreme Court decides cases as the High Court of Justice, it sits as a court of first instance, primarily reviewing decisions of government agencies and actors. Moreover, the court is characterized by accessibility, brevity, and low fees, characteristics that Dotan suggests would make the court attractive to have-nots. The heavy caseload of the court implies that Dotan is correct. From Galanter's perspective, this creates a situation where the risk to the one-shotter is much less than the risk to the repeat player, who could face a negative ruling that would serve as precedent in future cases. For Galanter's continuum, repeat players should seek greater numbers of settlements, and Dotan finds that they do. The results demonstrate that the haves enjoy considerable success before the Israeli High Court of Justice in litigation. Corporations won about 25 percent of cases, while individuals won about 10 percent. However, in out-of-court settlements, the have-nots succeeded at much higher rates, comparable to the success rates of corporations (almost 70 percent for have-nots compared to 65.5 percent for haves). Only in cases fully disposed of by the court did the haves enjoy a significant advantage over the have-nots. However, the success of various litigants appears to be affected by whether or not the petitioner has legal representation. Have-nots with an attorney fare much better than have-nots without, and the have-nots who have representation fare better than the haves. Because the government, the proto-typical repeat player, is always represented, the results suggest that legal representation can serve as an important intervention in the balance of power in high courts. Dotan's results align with Haynie's finding that courts may believe their legitimacy is affected by their rulings and view the institution as the "protector of the little person" (1999b, 1063).

Chan (2019) presents an interesting context for studying party capability theory. The study evaluates litigation in local courts in China, specifically focusing on 858 sampled judgments of rural land disputes between women who married individuals who did not reside in the village (married-out women, MOWs, and presumed have-nots) and the village collectives (the presumed haves). In these disputes the MOW litigants claiming access to land in the village won completely in 76.5 percent of the cases and won at least partially or completely in almost 94 percent of conflicts—an enviable if not astonishing record. Chan argues that, similar to Haynie's findings for the Philippine Supreme Court, the local courts in China "need to establish their legitimacy through adopting a redistributive policy when adjudicating MOW lawsuits" (15). Kim et al. (2021) analyze open government information requests to the Chinese government, the equivalent of freedom of information requests in the US context, and find that one-shotters are the most likely to file a request and are more successful when they do than repeat players who have filed multiple ones.

Also utilizing an interesting context, Bruijin and Vols (2020) find the opposite in their analysis of the decisions of Dutch lower courts in drug-related disputes brought by mayors (the "upperdogs") against property owners (the "underdogs"). Mayors enjoy the upper hand, and this proves especially so for mayors from larger cities. The authors do find one anomaly: mayors have a significantly lower chance against weak underdogs. Context matters for these disputes, and especially the type of drugs involved, as well as the defense invoked by the defendants.

Studying another interesting issue area, political corruption, Wu (2019b) does not find that those with superior resources, including political connections, consistently prevail in Taiwanese courts. Wu's analysis of district court verdicts from 2000 through 2015 involving corruption litigation finds only a limited advantage for party affiliation, political status, or the number of attorneys.

As noted by scholars of US courts, succeeding in court does not always equate to winning (Albiston 1999, 2003). Van Koppen and Malsch (1991) find that repeat players may prevail more frequently before judges in the Netherlands, but they have great difficulty collecting on their claims. The authors analyze all litigation for which a final decision was given among three of the nineteen Dutch trial courts in 1986. Corporate plaintiffs who succeeded in claims against individuals—that is, repeat players versus one-shotters—received lower proportions of the judgments issued in their favor. In 52 percent of the cases they received nothing within three years of the decision, and to gain any remuneration took longer against individuals and typically required additional writs or negotiation. Individual plaintiffs, however, collected 62 percent of the award when succeeding against corporations. While repeat players may win the legal battle, they "often lose in the collection war" (819). Repeat players of course may be concerned with symbolic victories that create favorable boundaries for future litigation. Winning the battles may be more critical for the war over the rules than collecting the spoils.

While studies of the Canadian Supreme Court find support for Galanter's thesis, Vidmar's (1984) study of the opposite end of the Canadian legal system, a small claims court, suggests that this venue offers an opportunity for one-shotters. Vidmar finds that repeat players "come out no better" than one-shotters, and especially when one considers the ability to actually collect on judgments.

While the formal legal system offers one avenue to resolve conflict, some comparative scholars study international tribunals tasked with resolving conflicts. Theoretically, we would expect, according to Galanter's thesis, that those nations with greater resources should prevail over those with fewer. Kopczynski (2008) tests Galanter's thesis by investigating the decisions of the World Trade Organization (WTO) through March 2007 and comparing litigated versus settled cases. In those cases decided by the WTO, "the average winner is typically the financial 'underdog'" (40). Even after removing the perennial repeat players that appear before the WTO, such as the US, countries with lower economic indicators still prevail. Kopczynski concludes that, at least for the WTO, "The haves come out behind" (47). The findings also indicate that the advantage of the have-nots has increased over the twelve years of the study, with greater success in the later years and less initially. This study suggests there are conflict resolution structures in which political and economic factors can temper the advantages that accrue to the haves, and that this moderation can be molded over time. Conversely, Conti (2010) finds that repeat participation tilts the playing field in favor of frequent litigators such as Canada, Brazil, and India. Over time, it becomes increasingly difficult for other players to "overcome the expertise gap" (659).

Like their US-focused colleagues, scholars of other legal systems have also applied Galanter's thesis to alternative dispute resolution processes. Gilad (2010) examines the British "private Ombudsman" process, examining 143 disputes between 2001 to 2004 that were resolved alternatively via this route. The author finds that firms' resources do not appear to significantly advantage them in outcomes. Gilad suggests that the nonbinding and informal nature of the process limits the ability of repeat players to strategically utilize this structure. Additionally, at least for this alternative dispute resolution process, prior experience does not seem to be the advantage that is demonstrated in analyses of the US arbitration system.

Lawyers as Repeat Players

Like scholars of the US legal system, researchers have spent substantial effort assessing the influence of legal representation, producing a number of studies, some already discussed in this chapter. This section examines studies where legal representation is the primary focus.

Flemming and Krutz (2002a, 2002b) review the effect of experienced advocates before the Canadian Supreme Court on the agenda-setting process. Their analysis of the applications for leave to appeal before the court from 1993 to 1995 indicate that litigant status, especially the government, has a significant effect on the probability of the court granting the appeal and hearing the petition. In addition, whether or not the applicant's advocate is Queen's Counsel, an honorific granted those with greater stature in the profession and presumably greater capability, does not appear to increase the likelihood of the appeal being accepted, contrary to expectations. Moreover, more experienced advocates are actually less likely to have their appeals granted. The mixed results provide some support for the proposition that repeat players are more likely to gain access to the court's agenda, but the role of the lawyer as a repeat player is not supported. Ultimately, with the exception of the government as the gorilla in the appeal process, the authors do not find substantial support for party capability theory. The authors suggest that the leave process in Canada, in which the Supreme Court entertains significantly fewer appeals than its US counterpart, may be partly to blame for the findings. The authors argue that because fewer requests are processed, the justices and their clerks have a greater ability to review the cases independent of the arguments proffered by counsel. In contrast, the US Supreme Court may view a repeat player attorney attached to a certiorari petition as a cue for case salience. Ultimately, these factors "diminish the impact of repeat players" in agenda setting before the Canadian Supreme Court (Flemming and Krutz 2002b, 833).[6]

While Flemming and Krutz are concerned with "deciding to decide" (2002a, 238), Szmer, Johnson, and Sarver (2007) focus on litigation outcomes before the Canadian Supreme Court from 1988 to 2000. Contrary to Flemming and Krutz, the authors find that appellants represented by advocates with greater litigation experience and those with larger litigation teams have a greater likelihood of winning. Similar to Flemming and Krutz, the authors find no effect for whether or not the advocate enjoys Queen's Counsel designation. They also confirm Flemming and Krutz's finding that more capable parties succeed, and that the government drives that finding. It should be noted that the authors also find an effect for ideology. Subsequent analysis by Kaheny, Szmer, and Sarver (2011) finds that legal teams dominated by women have a greater probability of success before the Supreme Court of Canada.

Haynie and Sill (2007) analyze the extent to which legal representation may affect the likelihood of success in the South African context. They evaluate whether or not more experienced advocates had greater success before the Appellate Division, the highest court of appeal prior to the creation of the Constitutional Court in 1994. They find that repeated appearances before the court did not increase the likelihood of success, but more capable attorneys did. After calculating the number of times the petitioner's advocate appears before the court compared to that of the respondent, they find no effect. However, when they compare the success rate of the petitioner's advocate to that of the respondent, they find an increased likelihood to prevail, even after controlling for litigant status. The authors do not suggest that resources are not relevant but that "the advantage that accrues to those with greater resources is not simply to procure a repeat player but to procure an advocate from the pool of repeat players who has had repeated success" (450).

Sheehan and Randazzo (2012) similarly find that the prior success of barristers before the Australian High Court is significantly related to future success. Simply appearing repeatedly may be insufficient to garner any advantage for a particular client, but securing a repeatedly successful advocate can increase the likelihood that a litigant, regardless of status, will prevail. This finding is also confirmed by Sheehan, Gill, and Randazzo (2012).

Lawyers also appear critical in an analysis of economic activity in Russia. In a 1997 survey of 328 Russian repeat players from the industrial sector, Hendley, Murrell, and Ryterman (1999, 2003) find that Russian repeat players behave much less predictably than Galanter's thesis suggests. They are less likely to play for the rules, are less likely to aggressively or innovatively mobilize resources, and are not reluctant to use the courts against other Russian repeat players. Lawyers are the persistently significant variable in predicting litigation activity, even though lawyers are seen as far less instrumental in economic development in Russia compared to the US. The authors see the evolving role of lawyers in Russia as critical to understanding the differences between the behavior of Russian repeat players and Galanter's prototypical repeat players. Lawyers are seen as technicians and less concerned with leveraging the advantages their employers enjoy in the Russian legal system.

Chen, Huang, and Lin (2014) find that the haves generally enjoy an advantage in both the quantity and the quality of legal talent when litigating before the Taiwanese Supreme Court. The authors find that an experienced attorney can affect the agenda-setting stage of the court, but in general, as Galanter predicts, appellants with higher status are more likely to win. The advantage enjoyed by the haves in Taiwan's judicial outcomes is further confirmed in Wu's (2019a) analysis of public land usurpation trial court litigation between 2000 and 2014. In both criminal and civil suits, the higher-status litigants win more often. In particular, government agencies, private sector litigants, and public offices win more often in trials involving usurpation of state-owned land. The results are less robust for criminal cases, but overall, Wu finds support for Galanter's thesis that the haves win.

Lawyers also develop "process expertise" (Kritzer 1998) that can positively affect outcomes. As Galanter notes, attorneys' expertise, developed over time as they navigate the legal system, can benefit their clients. Muro et al. (2018) confirm a "representational advantage" in their study of the decisions of the Supreme Court of Argentina. Their analysis of both decisions to dismiss appeals on formal grounds and decisions made after substantive review finds that lawyers familiar with the federal system have a distinct advantage. Conversely, Castelliano de Vasconcelos, Watanabe, and Netto (2018) find the opposite for outcomes in civil cases tried by federal attorneys in over 30,000 civil case outcomes in Brazil. They find no effect of attorney experience on the likelihood to succeed before Brazilian judges.

Paralleling analyses of alternative processes in the US context, Gazal-Ayal and Perry's (2014) analysis of Israeli labor courts' small claims settlements reveals that the probability of a successful settlement conference increases if the plaintiff has representation. However, whether the defendant was represented by a repeat player or a one-shotter does not affect outcomes. Most critically, the ratio between the sum claimed and the sum obtained was higher when the plaintiff was represented.

In their analysis of interest group participation across eleven English-speaking high courts from 1969 to 2002, Collins and McCarthy (2017) find that interest groups prefer participation in courts with the power of judicial review and that third-party participation rules across high courts constrain participation.

Government as Gorilla

As the prior chapter demonstrates, the government does indeed seem to loom large, and successfully so, in the American legal system, though with some variation in certain contexts and for certain issues. Scholars studying other nation states have similarly found variations on the theme of the government gorilla (Kritzer 2003).

If Galanter's thesis is universal, we would expect the government's advantage to be especially large in the criminal courts. Hagan (1982) interviewed litigants involved in criminal prosecutions in 1,000 randomly drawn criminal cases from 1976 and 1977 in Toronto, Canada. Hagan focuses on criminal cases in which corporate entities, including corporations, churches, associations, unions, and schools, "enlist the criminal law to prosecute and convict individuals who commit crimes against them" (994). Hagan then seeks to determine whether or not a corporate advantage exists in the criminal sphere. Hagan's thesis is an interesting one that complicates Galanter's picture a bit. Here, the one-shotter, the criminal defendant, faces two repeat players in a criminal court—the government and the corporation pressing for reparation of some sort. In addition to studying the criminal case dispositions, the author also conducted post-disposition interviews with individuals and corporations and discovered that approximately two-thirds of the victims in the sample were corporations and one-third were individuals. More telling for the author's purposes, almost 80 percent of crimes against corporations led to a conviction, while just over 65 percent of individual victims' cases resulted in a judgment of guilty. In general, the results provide support for the overall conclusion that "size is a reflection of power and resources" (1011).

McCormick (1993) focuses on the Canadian Supreme Court's decisions from 1949 to 1992. He tests Galanter's party capability theory by analyzing the success of differing litigants over time. McCormick sees judicial decisions, and especially the decisions of appellate courts, as an important resource over which parties compete but, like Shapiro and Kritzer, argues that the playing field on which the competition ensues is not a level one. His results confirm this assertion. The Crown enjoys a combined success rate as appellant and respondent of 67 percent, while the federal government succeeds at 62 percent, big business at 57 percent, and municipal governments at 54 percent, while the least successful among litigants are individuals, with a combined success rate as plaintiff and respondent of 44 percent. McCormick's results are an impressive confirmation of Galanter's thesis, but he does not address whether or not these success rates have shifted over time, as a number of US scholars have. He recognizes this limitation and acknowledges that leadership, procedural changes, and more liberal legal doctrine in the latter years of the analysis could lead to differing results across time. Nonetheless, he suggests that the results demonstrate a "persistent pattern of advantage" for the haves in the Supreme Court of Canada (540). In a further analysis of the decisions of the Canadian Supreme Court, Songer et al. (2012) confirm McCormick's results. The authors find a persistent advantage for the provincial and federal governments, which win 62 percent of their challenges before the high court. However, the authors find that individuals have greater success over businesses, contrary to McCormick's persistent pattern of advantage for the haves.

Atkins (1991) turns his focus to the English legal system, testing party capability using the decisions of the English Court of Appeal. While most analyses focus on either trial courts or the highest courts of appeal in the legal systems, Atkins studies the intermediate appellate court in the English system, which consists of some twenty-two lord justices of appeal. He specifically focuses on the decisions of these justices from 1983 to 1985 and evaluates the various one-shotter versus repeat player litigant interactions that Galanter proposes. Atkins finds substantial support for Galanter's expectations. The government is more likely to win when challenging or being challenged by a corporation, and most likely to win when challenged by an individual. The government's advantage continues when challenging an individual, but the advantage is less. Individuals also lose when challenging corporations. The results confirm Atkins's hypotheses and hold true when legal issues and legal rights are controlled for. The English Court of Appeal appears to mirror the US context.

Analyses extending Atkins's work find less overall support for Galanter's repeat player versus one-shotter thesis. Hanretty's (2014) study of appeals before the House of Lords from 1969 to 2003 does confirm Atkins's finding that the government enjoys significant advantages over other parties, but there are no advantages for businesses and associations over individuals. It should be noted that in addition to the government's advantage, the relative experience of the legal counsel in each case was also found to be significantly related to positive outcomes.

Alarie and Green (2017) focus primarily on the individual judge vote in their comparative analysis of the effect of high court design on outcomes. While their research question differs from ours, they do include an examination of government success in Canada, the US, the UK, India, and Australia. The authors find that the government enjoys the greatest measure of success as both appellant and respondent in the US and Canada. They find that "the 'Resources Matter' story does not really play out in the other countries" (202).

Institutional structures or processes can also skew outcomes to advantage the government. Skiple, Bentsen, and McKenzie's (2021) study of tax decisions in the Norwegian and Danish Supreme Courts finds that the government is less likely to win if justices have discretionary control of their docket and more likely to win if they do not. Individuals have much less success against the government when justices hear the case under a mandatory docket.

Eisenberg, Fisher, and Rosen (2011) explore the appellate jurisdiction of Israel's Supreme Court. Unlike Dotan's analysis of out-of-court settlements, the authors find a strong tendency to favor the government. For appeals involving mandatory review of criminal cases, the government succeeds over 80 percent of time. In mandatory review of civil cases, the results do not support a "consistent pro-corporate effect" in the court's decisions. Corporate plaintiffs who appeal losses from lower courts encounter an affirmance rate of almost 90 percent. Corporate defendants fare somewhat better but still succeed less than half the time. While the government appears to have significant support from the court, other repeat players do not.

Shvets's (2016) study of Russian *arbitrazh* courts, which handle economic disputes, analyzes the effect of a change in the judicial selection process on outcomes. In 1995 the appointment process shifted and more directly included presidential input in the selection of judges. Those appointed following the 1995 change are more likely to favor the government. Shvets finds that the probability of a firm winning against the government before a judge appointed with presidential preference is reduced by about 50 percent.

The advantage the Russian government enjoys in economic disputes is confirmed by Dzmitryieva, Titaev, and Chetverikovas (2016). The authors study a random sample of 10,000 cases resolved before Russian arbitrazh trial courts from 2007 to 2011 and find that in administrative disputes with entrepreneurs, the state wins an impressive 61.4 percent of the time. Interestingly, this advantage dissipates in civil cases, with the state winning only one-third of the time when challenging entrepreneurs.

In civil defamation suits in China, the government wins 73 percent of cases when suing the media. He and Lin's (2017) study of 524 defamation cases from 1993 to 2013 finds that over time, the media's success rate has been increasing, but the government has the greatest measure of success, especially when compared to the 46 percent success rate of media when sued by corporations and 47 percent when sued by ordinary individuals. While the authors find evidence of local protectionism, it is less than that found by other scholars, and especially for an issue area focused on freedom of the press in the Chinese context.

Bagashka and Tiede (2021) study the success of a particular type of repeat player, the procurator general, before the Bulgarian Constitutional Court. Similar to the American solicitor general but with powers broader in scope and function, the procurator general has a higher probability of winning before Bulgaria's highest court of appeal. Indeed, the authors find that judges are 56 percent more likely to align with the prosecutor general's preference in cases involving constitutional review.

Haynie's (2003) analysis of South Africa suggests that concerns for legitimacy may motivate appellate courts to temper their support for authoritarian regimes. Her analysis of the apartheid-era high court reveals that the Appellate Division, the highest court of appeal during the apartheid era, responded to its political environment. The court was required to interpret and enforce the antidemocratic and oppressive laws that were the foundation of the National Party's rule. Little confidence was placed in the court's ability to serve as a protector of individual rights (Corder and Davis 1989), and examinations of the major cases before the court provide little evidence that they did (Cameron 1982; Dyzenhaus 1998; Ellmann 1992), though others find greater support for underdogs (Abel 1995; Dugard 1978). Haynie finds that the decisions favoring the government declined in response to significant political events, such as the murder of popular activist Steve Biko or the Soweto riots. Indeed, the government's success increased during the initial years of the apartheid regime but declined concomitantly with its demise over the next forty years. Moreover, Haynie finds that from 1950 to 1990, individuals, corporations, and the government had similar overall success rates. In addition, individuals won half the challenges to apartheid regulations. She notes that the government won the major cases brought before the court, but in the more routine challenges of pass book violations and the like, individuals won one out of every two times. While the government consistently maintained a slightly higher rate of success when challenging or challenged by individuals and corporations, it certainly is not the advantage Galanter predicts.

Resources, Litigants, and Outcomes

In this chapter we compared the empirical analyses for the US courts to those focused on other countries. While much of the research confirms Galanter's party capability theory, there is variation in the strength and persistence of the confirmation. We seek to increase our understanding of the effects of resources on litigation outcomes by analyzing multiple countries with differing political, economic, and legal contexts across a significant period of time. Moreover, by including a variety of issues as well as varying contexts, we believe we will be better able to answer more confidently the question of why the haves do—or do not—come out ahead.

3 | Winners and Losers
An Aggregate Analysis

GALANTER SUGGESTS THAT those with greater resources, such as experience in the legal system, the ability to procure legal talent, and the ability to shape legal rules that protect their interests, should fare better in litigation outcomes. In practice, this means that poorer individuals who pursue claims against wealthier opponents should fail. Day in and day out across the globe, repeat players such as banks, insurance companies, hospitals, and doctors are challenged by or challenge one-shotters, typically individuals defending themselves in creditor-debtor disputes or delictual claims or contests of contracts.

Galanter argues that many one-shot, have-not litigants, such as private individuals, lack the ability to pick and choose their fights. Typically, individuals turn to litigation as a last resort for resolving conflicts when other avenues have failed, and for most, it may be the only legal conflict of their life. By contrast, repeat players are able to pick and choose their fights to establish rules that help them in subsequent conflicts. In essence, this was the problem that faced Patricia Johnson, Margaret Hennesy, Ronald Lucas, and others who owned modest homes in a previously all-residential area on the Isle of Dogs. This small peninsula in East London is surrounded on three sides by the river Thames and on the fourth by the West India Docks, built in 1802. Bananas and sugar cane from the West Indies and the Canary Islands were stored in the dock's large warehouse, which came to be known as Canary Wharf. The wharf's business expanded to include the majority of fruit and vegetable imports from South Africa and New Zealand. It continued to function through the 1960s, employing about 20,000 workers. Dwarfed by the new Port of London Authority's modern facilities downriver, Canary Wharf closed in 1981 (Fainstein 1994, 197).

The "Docklands" where Patricia, Margaret, and Ronald resided has long been an area inhabited by some of the poorest of Londoners. In 1982, hoping to revitalize the area, the Conservative government designated 482 acres of the Isle of Dogs as an enterprise zone. This designation freed developers from local planning regulations and also provided relief from a variety of property and business taxes. Despite opposition from the local boroughs, Olympia and York, a New York–based company that had successfully developed the World Financial Center, stepped in and promised to build a total of 11.6 million square feet of floor space (Fainstein 1994, 199). The Thatcher government praised the creation of a financial center in the Docklands area, but Patricia, Margaret, Ronald, and others were far less enthused.

While the Olympia and York venture collapsed, subsequent developers, Canary Wharf Ltd. and the London Docklands Development Corporation, completed the project, ultimately constructing a large (over 250 meters high and 50 meters square) building on previously vacant land that lay directly between the homeowners—including Patricia, Margaret, and Ronald—and the only British Broadcasting Company (BBC) transmitter that serviced the neighborhood. The residents, who on average watched twenty-four hours of television weekly, argued that the ability to receive television signals free from interference was so important to the enjoyment of a householder that any interference with those signals should be regarded as a legal nuisance.[1] After all, obstructing access to the local news, if not episodes of television favorites such as *Dr. Who, Mr. Bean,* and the original *House of Cards,* surely constitutes tortious conduct.

The evidence was overwhelming that the construction of the building was the primary and proximate cause of the interference, which began during construction in 1989 and continued for several years until the BBC built a relay transmitter. Unfortunately for the residents, the corporate defendants were able to rely on several precedents established in earlier litigation initiated by other corporations to win their case. These precedents reinforce Galanter's contention that the law is rarely neutral but instead often supports the interests of the haves rather than the interests of the have-nots. First, the court cited a 1965 ruling which held that such interference with television reception did not constitute a legal nuisance because it was interference with a purely recreational facility, as opposed to interference with the health or well-being of the plaintiffs.[2] The court then cited a nineteenth-century decision that, as a general rule, "a man is entitled to build on his own land," though nowadays this right is inevitably subject to planning controls.[3] Still, as a general rule, a man's right to build on his land is not restricted by the fact that the presence of the building may of itself interfere with a neighbor's enjoyment of his or her land.

The court noted that occasionally, activities on a homeowner's land can be so offensive to neighbors as to constitute an actionable nuisance; for example, the persistent view of prostitutes and their clients entering and leaving neighboring premises was held to fall into that category.[4] However, the court concluded that such cases must, of necessity, be relatively rare. Therefore the court refused to apply the precedent of the unwanted prostitutes to the present case of the unwanted blockage of television reception. Because existing law strongly privileged the rights of commercial landowners over the rights of their neighbors, the court concluded that objections to potential nuisances had to be brought to the attention of the local planning authority at the stage of the application for planning permission. Since no such objection was raised by the neighbors prior to the building at issue in this case, the court concluded that the rights of the owners of the building must prevail. The court did note that it is quite possible that the problem may not have been anticipated until after the building was built, when it was too late for any such representations to be made. However, the court concluded that there was no obligation on the part of the building's owners to hire experts to evaluate potential effects on the neighbors, given the freedom of the neighbors to hire whatever experts they wished to evaluate the building's effects once the building plans were announced. In effect, the court indicated that the lack of resources on the part of one of the litigants to pay for the expert help needed to protect their interests did not excuse their failure to make the timely challenge that the existing law required. Thus, as Galanter suggests, one of the advantages of the haves is their continuing access to talented legal help not available to their have-not opponents, an advantage that may essentially determine the outcome of future litigation before that litigation is formally launched. Ironically, the court seems to have ignored the fact that the national government in its efforts to promote economic development allowed Canary Wharf Ltd. and the London Docklands Development Corporation to bypass local planning authorities and ignore any local zoning ordinances or restrictions. Even if Patricia, Margaret, and Ronald had foreseen their inability to enjoy the award-winning antics of Rowan Atkinson, the establishment of the enterprise zone precluded their intervention during the planning process.

Once formal litigation is begun, the haves often are advantaged by having superior legal representation. The corporate defendants were represented by Lord Derry Irvine of Lairg, QC, one of the most politically well-connected barristers in the country. He had been Queen's Counsel for twenty years prior to the present case and, as a frequent instructor in one of the prominent inns of the court, counted both Tony Blair (the prime minister of the UK at the time of the dispute) and Cherrie Booth (wife of the prime minister) among his barrister pupils, the former appointing him lord chancellor after his election as prime minister in 1997.[5]

Large corporate interests like Canary Wharf Ltd. represent the types of repeat players that Galanter envisioned winning repeatedly in courts of law. Another prototypical repeat player is the insurance corporation. Insurance companies are involved in litigation on a regular basis. Claims are denied, and individuals may decide they have few options to obtain redress other than litigation. Moreover, the potential to secure large settlements and, in most countries, the legal fees associated with them allows one-shotters to obtain legal counsel that might balance the scales. Nonetheless, according to Galanter's thesis, the ability of corporate interests to shape the rules should still ensure that their preferences prevail. Such a battle between a have insurance company and a have-not insured began innocently enough with a camping trip in February 1991.[6]

On February 16, 1991, Andrew Johnson was camping in Australia's Blackwood National Park near Sue's Bridge. The bridge was built in 1966 and crosses the Blackwood River, one of the longest rivers in Western Australia, girded on each side by a canopy of the lush green jarrah forest and the smaller, more accessible peppermint trees of its understory. Around the limb of one of these trees Mr. Johnson discovered a rope and was tempted by the lure of its trajectory, sure to plunge him into the cold waters of the Blackwood River. Unfortunately for Mr. Johnson, the rope gave way as he swung toward the water, and he crashed to the ground, injuring his right foot. The resulting fractures were so severe that the orthopedic surgeon recommended amputation, convinced that the loss of mobility Mr. Johnson would suffer, as well as the accompanying pain, necessitated such a course of action. Mr. Johnson, however, was much less enthusiastic about losing his foot. Even four years after the injury, surgeons were deliberating whether amputation was "inevitable" or merely "probable." It appears that the physicians, as well as the lower court judge, accepted that at some point, Mr. Johnson would undergo amputation of his foot, even if Mr. Johnson did not.

Unlike many individuals who face such devastating injuries, Mr. Johnson had presciently procured an insurance policy that promised to pay if Mr. Johnson had an injury that resulted in the total loss of a foot at or above the ankle that, after twelve months, was beyond hope of improvement. Here is where the legal dispute arises. Mr. Johnson argued he clearly had a total loss of the use of his foot; the insurance company disagreed. Mr. Johnson stood to recover $500,000 if it was determined that he had a "permanent total loss of use of one limb."

The legal disagreement revolved around the loss of the foot "as a foot," and the factual dispute concerning this loss pitted the physicians on one side against the insurance company on the other. The physicians testified that the appellant could stand and walk on both legs without crutches but did so with pain, sometimes severe. Much of the bone in the heel had been removed, and the big toe joint was "markedly" stiff. With a specially built orthotic Mr. Johnson could walk for about 100 meters "on . . . a good day," but without the orthotic he was unable to walk at all. The insurance company, on the other hand, argued that Mr. Johnson's foot was functioning quite well, sufficient to enable him to walk unaided. Unbeknownst to Mr. Johnson, the company had videotaped him walking and squatting in a garden without crutches or walking sticks, and with no trace of a limp. Such evidence was clear proof that Mr. Johnson had not lost the use of his foot, they argued.

Not so, countered Mr. Johnson. His ability to navigate the garden was dependent on the orthotic and the videotape happened to catch a moment when Mr. Johnson had less pain and more energy. Even if he appeared to be sufficiently mobile, he had no use of the foot "as a foot," but was dependent on the insert. The lower court judge ruled that it was appropriate to consider the function of the foot with the orthotic, and thus the injury necessarily fell outside the meaning of the policy's "total permanent loss" of the limb.

The High Court of Australia was left to determine whether Mr. Johnson had lost the use of his foot or whether he was only required now to use the insert in order to use his foot. Inconvenient, perhaps, uncomfortable or even painful, but did such support constitute the equivalent of, say, pain medication for severe headaches? Mr. Johnson argued that the inability to use the foot without orthotics meant he had lost the use of his foot and was owed the compensation guaranteed in the policy.

According to the lower court judge, "The use to which the plaintiff has put, and continues to put, his foot could be said to be so 'unreasonable' or 'impractical' as not to amount to a 'use' at all." Appeal to a full bench of the lower court resulted in a similar conclusion that the use of the orthotics was immaterial. Mr. Johnson was able "to walk, to stand, to bear weight, to walk backwards and to squat" with "the simple expedient of an insert." To suggest that he therefore had lost the use of his foot would be the same as suggesting that a man who could see perfectly well with glasses had lost his sight if he could not function without them.

The majority of the High Court sided with the American Home Assurance Company. The justices argued that the policy was written in "plain English" and similar to policies issued daily across not just Australia but the globe. The court was not interested in reviewing the videotaped evidence itself but did rely on the lower court's evaluation of it. Moreover, the court agreed with the full bench that the correct understanding of "total permanent loss" would require that Mr. Johnson had lost his ability to walk on the foot with or without an insert. However, Mr. Johnson found one sympathetic ear on the court in Justice Kirby, who noted in his dissent the guarantee of Psalm 91, that the angels shall "bear thee up in their hands, lest thou dash thy foot against a stone." Unfortunately, as Justice Kirby noted, neither the heavenly angels nor the earthly American Home Assurance Company intervened to aid Mr. Johnson. From Justice Kirby's understanding of the plain meaning, loss should mean loss, not loss unless an aid can correct the loss. The justice found similarities to an Alabama Supreme Court case in which an individual could not walk or stand without pain and used two canes for mobility. For Justice Kirby, "without express provision in the policy," loss of use must mean "loss of unassisted use of the limb in question, i.e. without supplementation by external objects." Justice Kirby did not ignore the videotaped evidence that demonstrated Mr. Johnson's mobility, at least for the period of time captured on tape, but argued that the trial judge erred in excluding the orthotic from the evaluation. Justice Kirby would have remanded the case to the lower court to determine whether or not, absent any supplemental aids, Mr. Johnson had indeed lost the use of his foot—as a foot. Unfortunately for Mr. Johnson, the lesser angels of the court disagreed, and not only was his foot dashed against the stone, his ability to recover compensation was as well.

Galanter's hypothesis would have accurately predicted the outcome in both these cases. One-shotters faced repeat players with the resources, time, and patience to prevail. While case studies such as these are instructive, more critical is the need to evaluate winners and losers across multiple courts with both comparability and sufficient variation to test Galanter's theory empirically. As the previous chapters demonstrate, scholars have examined the success of the haves in a number of contexts, and the results provide some support for Galanter's thesis, but that support has not provided a truly comparative empirical test of party capability theory.

Few scholars have attempted to replicate the methods used to analyze the courts in previous single-nation studies into a comparative analysis. Thus we have neither truly comparative empirical analyses of the role of courts nor a series of single-nation case studies that attempted to apply a common methodology, and none that does so over a significant period of time. The data for the analyses are drawn from the National High Courts Database.[7] This database allows us to address the shortcomings in the literature in three ways. First, the database uses a common coding scheme across each of the six courts included in the analysis. The data set provides the only cross-country data with common variables, including litigants, issues, and outcomes, among other variables of interest for us. The data set includes the universe of cases annually from 1970 to 2000 for Australia (1,893), Canada (1,565), the UK (3,216), and South Africa (2,385), and a random sample of approximately 100 cases each year for India (3,216) and the Philippines (3,066), where their highest courts of appeal decide 1,200 to more than 1,800 cases annually. In total, 15,211 appellate court decisions are included in the data. In addition, in order to make the findings as comparable as possible to existing party capability studies from other countries, the operational definitions of litigant classifications, outcomes, and issues were designed to be congruent with earlier analyses of Canada (McCormick 1993; Songer 2008), the Philippines (Haynie 1994, 1995), South Africa (Haynie 2003), the US courts of appeals (Songer and Sheehan 1992), and the US Supreme Court (Sheehan, Mishler, and Songer 1992), among others. Finally, we conduct our analysis over a lengthy period of time to prevent inferences that may be due to a single data point.

As Wheeler et al. (1987) point out in their analysis of state supreme courts, specific information about the wealth or other resources of particular parties in a given case often is not available in court opinions. We found this absence of information about litigant resources to be a characteristic of the opinions in all the countries that we studied as well. Since our data are also derived from court opinions, we often are not able unambiguously to classify one of the litigants as having greater litigation resources than its opponent. Consequently, we adopt the strategy utilized in most previous party capability studies (e.g., McCormick 1993; Songer and Sheehan 1992; Wheeler et al. 1987) of assigning litigants to general categories and then making assumptions about which class usually has greater litigation resources. Litigants were classified into four categories: national government (including its agencies and officials), other government agencies and officials, businesses (including corporations) and associations (e.g., unions, interest groups, churches, other groups), and individuals. We assume that on average, the national government has the greatest litigation resources, subnational governments have the second-greatest average resources, businesses and groups would be third, and individuals usually have the fewest resources.[8] Like Wheeler et al. (1987) and Songer and Sheehan (1992), we assume that when business and government litigate, the government usually will be stronger because even when the financial resources of government are no greater than those of business, the government agency is more likely to be a repeat player or at least a more frequent repeat player in the particular issue area involved in the suit.

Following the approach of Wheeler et al. (1987), which was later adopted by Songer and Sheehan (1992), McCormick (1993), and Haynie (1994), among others, we define winners and losers by looking at "who won the appeal in its most immediate sense, without attempting to view the appeal in some larger context" (Wheeler et al. 1987, 415). Thus, for example, if the decision of a provincial appellate court to award damages to an individual allegedly injured by his employer is "reversed" or "vacated" or "reversed and remanded" by the national high court, the appellant (i.e., the business employer) is coded as winning. If in this same hypothetical case the national high court affirmed the decision of the provincial court, dismissed the appeal, or concluded that the appeal could not be allowed, the respondent individual would be coded as winning. Cases in which the winner could not be determined unambiguously (e.g., most of the decisions in which the decision of the lower court was affirmed in part and reversed in part) were excluded from analysis.

As in the earlier studies of party capability, our focus is on whether any relative advantage accrues to those classes of litigants with superior litigation resources and whether, if a relative advantage exists, it varies across countries. Appeals are brought by litigants who have already lost at least once in the lower courts. Therefore, even if appellate justice is blind and litigation resources are irrelevant, one would expect respondents to prevail in the majority of appeals (Songer and Sheehan 1992, 240). In fact, a cursory examination of the data from our countries indicates that the respondents do win at a greater rate than appellants (55 percent to 40 percent). Therefore, to assess whether the hypothesized relative advantage of litigants with superior resources exists, it is not enough to know which class of litigants won more often in an absolute sense. The overall success rate of a given class of litigants can be expected to be influenced by how frequently they appear before the national high court as the appellant rather than as a respondent. We must also know whether a given class of litigants is "better able than other parties to buck the basic tendency of appellate courts to affirm" (Wheeler et al. 1987, 407). To measure this aspect of relative advantage a number of studies (McCormick 1993; Songer and Sheehan 1992; Wheeler et al. 1987) have computed an "index of net advantage."

This index is computed for each litigant class by taking the class members' success rate when they appear as appellant and from that figure subtracting the reversal rate when they appear as respondent (i.e., subtracting the success rate of their opponents). This index of advantage is independent of the relative frequency that different classes of litigants appear as appellants versus respondents. In addition, it is also independent of the relative propensity of different courts to affirm and is therefore a better measure to use in cross-court comparisons than a simple measure of the proportion of decisions won by a given class of litigants would be (Songer and Sheehan 1992, 241).

Table 1 reports the net advantage of different litigants before their highest courts. If one looks only at the overall net advantages across all six nations, the results would be consistent with Galanter's theory. Overall, individuals have the lowest net advantage, at −11 percent, corporations are at −9 percent, and associations are at −6 percent. The litigant with the greatest net advantage before high courts of appeal is in fact the government, as Galanter would predict, but the aggregate does not tell the full story.[9] What is most striking is that there is such variation in the high courts. Canada and the UK appear to adhere more closely to party capability theory. In the UK, the national government has the greatest net advantage, at 24 percent. Businesses have a higher net advantage than individuals but lower than associations, though the net advantage of businesses in the UK is considerably lower than that of the government. Individuals have the lowest net advantage; moreover, individuals in Canada and the UK are the least likely to succeed of any of the countries included in the analysis. Conversely, individuals before the Australian High Court have the only positive net advantage of any country, though it is certainly a very modest one. The government has a positive net advantage in Australia, but it is only 7 percent. The Philippine government has the lowest net advantage of any government, −14 percent, and corporations fare even worse—hardly the results that party capability theory would predict. In fact, individuals in the Philippines are more likely to succeed than corporations, with a net advantage of −26 percent compared to the −37 percent of corporations. In India, the government has the highest net advantage, while individuals fare worse than corporations but better than associations. South Africa presents an interesting case. The country was nondemocratic for twenty-four years of the analysis. Thus the bulk of the analysis is derived from rulings under the apartheid regime, yet the government of South Africa has only a slightly higher net advantage when compared to the individual (−1 percent net advantage for individuals to 2 percent net advantage for the government).

TABLE 1. Net advantage of parties before the high courts, 1970–2000 (%)

Type of party	Success rate as petitioner	When respondent, opponent's success rate	Net advantage	Averaged success rate (as petitioner and respondent)
Australia				
Individual	52	50	1	51
Corporation	43	45	−2	49
Association	35	54	−19	41
Government	55	48	7	53
Canada				
Individual	37	53	−16	42
Corporation	43	49	−6	47
Association	40	46	−6	47
Government	54	33	22	61
United Kingdom				
Individual	38	54	−16	42
Corporation	44	50	−6	47
Association	52	45	7	53
Government	57	33	24	62
India				
Individual	42	51	−9	45
Corporation	43	47	−4	48
Association	30	43	−14	43
Government	50	37	13	57
Philippines				
Individual	22	48	−26	37
Corporation	15	52	−37	32
Association	28	32	−4	48
Government	28	41	−14	43
South Africa				
Individual	42	43	−1	50
Corporation	38	40	−2	49
Association	39	38	0	50
Government	41	40	2	51

TABLE 1 (*continued*)

Type of party	Success rate as petitioner	When respondent, opponent's success rate	Net advantage	Averaged success rate (as petitioner and respondent)
Average				
Individual	38	50	−11	44
Corporation	38	47	−9	45
Association	37	43	−6	47
Government	47	38	9	55

The lowest net advantage belongs to corporations, but the differences among the four categories of litigants are negligible.

Table 2 provides the success rates of certain litigant interactions. The analysis reveals that the government has the greatest level of success in the Philippines when challenging individuals, at 62 percent. The UK follows, with a success rate of 59 percent when challenging individuals. The government of South Africa has the lowest success when challenging individuals, 43 percent, though Australia is only slightly higher, at 46 percent. The success rates of the governments of Canada and India are identical when they face individuals before their highest courts, 52 percent.

While the Australian government does not fare well against individuals, it has a much higher success rate against corporations, winning 64 percent of the cases in which the government challenges a corporation, the highest success rate of any government in that litigant interaction category. These results are consistent with other studies indicating a change in legal culture and legal structure that led to higher success rates for individuals when opposing the government (Sheehan, Gill, and Randazzo 2012; Sheehan and Randazzo 2012). In the other countries, the government has lower success rates when facing businesses in high courts, ranging from a low of 31 percent in the Philippines to 58 percent in Canada. With the exception of the Philippines, governments fare much better against associations, with a mean success rate across the six nations of 68 percent, though these results also reflect a small number of cases in every country.

Only in Australia and Canada do corporations have at least a 50 percent success rate as appellants in any litigant interaction. Corporations have the lowest success rates across the countries when they face the government, ranging from a low of 27 percent in the Philippines to a high of 44 percent in

TABLE 2. Petitioner success rates against different respondents before high courts, 1970–2000 (%)

Petitioner	Respondent (N)			
	Individual	Corporation	Association	Government
Australia				
Individual	49 (178)	49 (132)	61 (18)	51 (377)
Corporation	48 (99)	40 (172)	77 (17)	44 (94)
Association	50 (8)	31 (13)	33 (12)	30 (27)
Government	46 (74)	64 (52)	100 (1)	100 (1)
Canada				
Individual	51 (197)	49 (139)	39 (18)	31 (286)
Corporation	39 (119)	47 (257)	54 (26)	41 (98)
Association	43 (14)	48 (31)	29 (14)	16 (19)
Government	52 (98)	58 (60)	83 (6)	29 (7)
United Kingdom				
Individual	46 (109)	48 (96)	33 (15)	32 (238)
Corporation	46 (74)	49 (247)	40 (10)	32 (97)
Association	67 (6)	67 (9)	100 (1)	38 (8)
Government	59 (117)	49 (63)	71 (7)	
India				
Individual	50 (514)	54 (59)	33 (21)	39 (543)
Corporation	40 (81)	48 (50)	46 (13)	39 (104)
Association	55 (22)	64 (14)	20 (5)	13 (45)
Government	52 (150)	44 (55)	75 (8)	0 (5)
Philippines				
Individual	47 (446)	57 (49)	17 (6)	43 (366)
Corporation	38 (93)	47 (34)	28 (25)	27 (33)
Association	57 (14)	53 (19)	86 (7)	33 (12)
Government	62 (87)	31 (16)	11 (9)	33 (3)
South Africa				
Individual	46 (184)	46 (202)	23 (30)	40 (462)
Corporation	43 (227)	35 (334)	47 (17)	36 (103)
Association	40 (10)	38 (24)	38 (8)	56 (9)
Government	43 (120)	45 (80)	60 (10)	0 (1)

TABLE 2 (*continued*)

Petitioner	Respondent (N)			
	Individual	Corporation	Association	Government
Average				
Individual	48 (385)	50 (125)	34 (23)	39 (517
Corporation	42 (132)	44 (193)	49 (20)	36 (114)
Association	52 (18)	51 (22)	50 (9)	31 (30)
Government	52 (143)	48 (67)	68 (8)	32 (5)

Australia, but their success rate is only slightly higher when challenging individuals. These results parallel prior research demonstrating that the court is deferential to the have-not individuals, cognizant of the economic challenges facing ordinary citizens litigating before them (Haynie 1994, 1995; Tate and Haynie 1994). Corporations fare least well against individuals in the Philippines (38 percent), Canada (39 percent), and India (40 percent), but only marginally better in South Africa (43 percent), the UK (46 percent), and Australia (48 percent). Corporations experience the highest success rates against associations in Australia (77 percent) but do not do nearly as well against them in either the Philippines (28 percent) or the UK (40 percent).

Again, as in table 1, the results do not conform to the expectations that the party presumed to have the greater resources in court will prevail. There is significant variation in who wins and who loses in litigant interactions across our six nations.

Table 3 provides the net advantages (subtracting the respondent's success rate from the petitioner's success rate) for different combinations of parties. For example, in Australia, when the individual challenges the government, the individual's success rate is 51 percent, as shown in table 2. Table 2 also demonstrates that when the individual is a respondent challenged by the government in Australia, the individual's success rate is 46 percent. This creates an overall net advantage of 5 percent favoring individuals, which is reported in table 3. We use the success rates in table 2 to assess similar net advantages among different litigant interactions and report these in table 3. Overall, individuals fare much better than Galanter's thesis would predict when opposing or opposed by corporations. Individuals have the net advantage in these litigant interactions in every single country except India, where corporations enjoy a net advantage in litigant interactions with individuals of 14 percent,

TABLE 3. Net advantage for different combinations of parties (%)

Parties	Net Advantage
Australia	
Individual v. government	Individual by 5
Individual v. association	Individual by 11
Individual v. corporation	Individual by 9
Corporation v. government	Government by 20
Corporation v. association	Corporation by 46
Association v. government	Government by 70
Canada	
Individual v. government	Government by 19
Individual v. association	Association by 4
Individual v. corporation	Individual by 10
Corporation v. government	Government by 17
Corporation v. association	Corporation by 6
Association v. government	Government by 67
United Kingdom	
Individual v. government	Government by 27
Individual v. association	Association by 4
Individual v. corporation	Individual by 2
Corporation v. government	Government by 17
Corporation v. association	Association by 27
Association v. government	Government by 33
India	
Individual v. government	Government by 13
Individual v. association	Association by 22
Individual v. corporation	Corporation by 14
Corporation v. government	Government by 5
Corporation v. association	Association by 18
Association v. government	Government by 62
Philippines	
Individual v. government	Government by 19
Individual v. association	Association by 40
Individual v. corporation	Individual by 19
Corporation v. government	Government by 4
Corporation v. association	Association by 25
Association v. government	Association by 22

TABLE 3 *(continued)*

Parties	Net Advantage
South Africa	
Individual v. government	Government by 3
Individual v. association	Association by 17
Individual v. corporation	Individual by 3
Corporation v. government	Government by 9
Corporation v. association	Corporation by 9
Association v. government	Government by 4
Average	
Individual v. government	Government by 13
Individual v. association	Association by 18
Individual v. corporation	Individual by 8
Corporation v. government	Government by 11
Corporation v. association	Association by 1
Association v. government	Government by 36

but in Australia, Canada, the UK, the Philippines, and South Africa, individuals enjoy net advantages of 9 percent, 10 percent, 2 percent, 19 percent, and 3 percent, respectively. If individuals are able to reach the highest courts of appeal in these countries, their net advantage is 8 percent overall.

Conversely, the government fares best in every country but Australia, where the individual in litigant combinations involving the government enjoys a net advantage of 5 percent. The UK has the greatest net advantage, at 27 percent, followed by Canada and the Philippines, at 19 percent each, India, at 13 percent, and South Africa, at only 3 percent. While these results more closely reflect Galanter's paradigm, it is certainly not the overwhelming advantage one might have anticipated.

The highest net advantages arise in challenges between the government and associations, rising to 70 percent in Australia and 67 percent in Canada, followed by India (62 percent), the UK (33 percent), and South Africa (4 percent). Only in the Philippines do associations enjoy a net advantage when litigating with the government. The overall net advantage weighs heavily in favor of the government across all countries, with a 36 percent government net advantage.

Associations fare somewhat better when they oppose or are opposed by corporations. Their net advantage is 27 percent in the UK against litigant interactions with corporations, 25 percent in the Philippines, and 18 percent in India. Corporations have the net advantage in Australia (46 percent), Canada (6 percent), and South Africa (9 percent). The overall net advantage only slightly favors associations, with a 1 percent net advantage in their favor.

Associations have the strongest record of success when challenging or challenged by individuals, as Galanter would predict, with an overall net advantage across all six countries of 18 percent. Associations have the advantage in all but Australia, where the individual succeeds in 61 percent of cases in which they challenge associations but in only 50 percent of cases in which they are challenged by associations, for a net advantage of 11 percent.

However, this category also has the smallest number of cases, suggesting that across all the countries, associations rarely litigate as direct parties and succeed even more rarely. Organizations, associations, interest groups—all of which fall into this category—participate more frequently as intervenors. As in studies of US interest groups, it appears that associations participate in litigation, either as direct participants or as intervenors, less frequently than corporations, individuals, or the government. While such participation would presumably provide an advantage, in light of the general repeat player status of associations, the results suggest that when associations are direct participants, they can expect a distinct disadvantage when challenging the government, an advantage when interacting with individuals, and basically a 50/50 chance of success when challenging or being challenged by corporations. Corporations have the least success across all combinations of litigant interactions, succeeding only on occasion in certain countries, and in no combination do they experience a net advantage overall.

While tables 1, 2, and 3 provide a useful starting point for a cross-national comparison of party capability, it is possible that the results are confounded by differences in the issue agendas in each court. The success rates in different countries may have more to do with the docket composition than with litigation resources in general. To explore any bias in the cross-court comparisons that may result from agenda differences, we follow up our initial analysis with an examination of success rates for each category of litigants for five major categories of issues: criminal appeals, civil rights and liberties disputes, private economic disputes, tort cases, and public law cases. The category of criminal cases includes challenges to convictions, challenges to sentences, and appeals of pretrial procedural decisions in criminal cases. Civil rights and liberties appeals involve issues of equal protection, speech, press, assembly, petition, religious freedom, voting rights, rights to privacy, and the rights of Indigenous peoples. Private economic disputes include contract disputes, debt collection, disputes over real property, landlord-tenant disputes, labor relations, and corporate law issues. The public law category includes government regulation of the economy, environmental regulation, consumer protection, taxation, public employment, immigration, disputes between different levels or units of government, and disputes over government benefit programs. Tort appeals involve motor vehicle accidents, workplace injuries, medical or legal malpractice, product liability, and government tort liability.

Table 4 presents the success rate when the individual is the petitioner, the success rate when the individual is the respondent, the net advantage (subtracting the respondent's success rate from the petitioner's success rate), and the averaged success rate for the individual within issue categories across each country. If Galanter is correct that individuals, the typical one-shotters in courts of law and presumably even more so in appellate courts, are the least advantaged and therefore least likely to win, we would anticipate individuals exhibiting the lowest averaged success rates across all countries in all issue categories. The results do not support a conclusion that individuals are routinely disadvantaged in the highest courts of appeal, at least for some issue categories. In particular, individuals have positive net advantages for tort cases in Australia, Canada, India, and South Africa, private economic cases in Canada, and, most interestingly, a net advantage, though a small one, for public law cases in South Africa. Not surprisingly, individuals fare least well in criminal cases, but again, their averaged success rates vary considerably across these countries. In Australia and South Africa, individuals can expect to win about half the time when their success rates as petitioners and respondents are averaged. However, individuals have little success in criminal disputes in the UK, Canada, and especially the Philippines. For civil rights and liberties issues, individuals enjoy a positive net advantage only in South Africa, whose nondemocratic regime dominates the majority of the time frame for the analysis. Compare this to the Philippines, where Marcos's dictatorship spans approximately half of the thirty-one years under study, or the net advantage of individuals in India, a country whose states of emergency may have constrained the ability of individuals to succeed. Conversely, the imposition of Canada's Charter of Rights may have increased the ability of individuals to succeed in rights and liberties disputes, and the net advantage for individuals in such disputes, while still negative, is better than that in every other country but South Africa and Australia. Clearly, analyses that assess the effect of contractions or

TABLE 4. Net advantage for individual by issue (%)

Issue	Success rate as petitioner (N)	When respondent, opponents' success rate (N)	Net advantage	Averaged success rate (as petitioner and respondent)
Australia				
Criminal	51 (316)	51 (51)	0	50
Civil rights and liberties	48 (23)	54 (13)	−6	47
Private economic	38 (134)	42 (102)	−4	48
Torts	61 (163)	46 (126)	15	57
Public law	52 (136)	62 (84)	−0	45
United Kingdom				
Criminal	31 (221)	62 (100)	−31	34
Civil rights and liberties	46 (55)	52 (25)	−7	47
Private economic	40 (83)	51 (71)	−11	45
Torts	47 (99)	49 (92)	−2	49
Public law	33 (83)	56 (78)	−24	38
Canada				
Criminal	30 (888)	60 (296)	−30	35
Civil rights and liberties	37 (84)	50 (34)	−13	43
Private economic	50 (129)	46 (118)	5	52
Torts	53 (138)	46 (127)	7	54
Public law	43 (197)	49 (89)	−7	47
India				
Criminal	44 (426)	54 (117)	−10	45
Civil rights and liberties	22 (148)	52 (21)	−31	35
Private economic	48 (383)	48 (376)	0	50
Torts	65 (20)	41 (17)	24	62
Public law	40 (590)	53 (393)	−14	43
Philippines				
Criminal	10 (709)	59 (46)	−49	26
Civil rights and liberties	34 (62)	63 (27)	−29	35
Private economic	23 (562)	47 (289)	−24	38
Torts	30 (46)	42 (33)	−12	44
Public law	35 (321)	44 (123)	−9	46

TABLE 4 (*continued*)

Issue	Success rate as petitioner (N)	When respondent, opponents' success rate (N)	Net advantage	Averaged success rate (as petitioner and respondent)
South Africa				
Criminal	40 (382)	43 (35)	−3	49
Civil rights and liberties	50 (14)	48 (21)	2	51
Private economic	44 (234)	47 (232)	−4	48
Torts	45 (163)	36 (185)	9	54
Public law	39 (75)	38 (72)	1	51
Average				
Criminal	34 (578)	54 (132)	−20	40
Civil rights and liberties	39 (100)	54 (29)	−15	42
Private economic	41 (338)	47 (277)	−6	47
Torts	49 (109)	43 (99)	6	53
Public law	40 (378)	50 (233)	−11	45

expansions of democratic structures on success rates in these countries would be helpful. We explore this further in chapter 5.

Corporations do not fare as well as party capability theory would suggest. As is evident from table 5, on average, corporations fail to achieve a substantial positive net advantage in any issue category. In categories where one would assume repeat player status to advantage them, such as private economics and tort issues, corporations have a −6 percent overall net advantage in the former and a −20 percent net advantage in the latter.

Corporations fare better in Australia than in the other countries, with a positive net advantage in private economic cases of 3 percent and no net advantage or disadvantage in civil rights and liberties cases, a category where corporations have some but very few disputes. There are on average seven cases per country in which the corporation is the petitioner and on average nine per country in which the corporation is the respondent. When corporations bring challenges to public laws, they also do not have a distinct advantage. Only in India do corporations enjoy a modest positive net advantage.

Table 6 provides the success rates as petitioner and respondent for associations, along with their net advantage before the highest courts of appeal across the six countries under study. Associations participate most often in challenges to public laws, and do so most frequently in India and Canada,

TABLE 5. Net advantage for corporation by issue (%)

Issue	Success rate as petitioner (N)	When respondent, opponents' success rate (N)	Net advantage	Averaged success rate (as petitioner and respondent)
Australia				
Civil rights and liberties	75 (8)	75 (4)	0	50
Private economic	44 (204)	40 (229)	3	52
Torts	35 (79)	48 (98)	−13	44
Public law	46 (144)	58 (85)	−12	44
United Kingdom				
Civil rights and liberties	22 (9)	63 (16)	−40	30
Private economic	50 (232)	50 (250)	0	50
Torts	46 (115)	47 (117)	−1	50
Public law	33 (88)	52 (62)	−19	41
Canada				
Civil rights and liberties	54 (13)	67 (18)	−13	44
Private economic	44 (308)	45 (308)	−1	49
Torts	47 (90)	56 (101)	−10	45
Public law	42 (173)	50 (96)	−8	46
India				
Civil rights and liberties	50 (2)	100 (1)	−50	25
Private economic	46 (144)	51 (121)	−5	47
Torts	38 (16)	83 (6)	−46	27
Public law	42 (253)	40 (17)6	1	51
Philippines				
Civil rights and liberties	33 (3)	67 (3)	−33	33
Private economic	16 (344)	51 (78)	−35	33
Torts	8 (39)	50 (6)	−42	29
Public law	12 (67)	48 (31)	−37	32
South Africa				
Civil rights and liberties	0 (2)	40 (5)	−40	30
Private economic	39 (495)	38 (464)	1	50
Torts	34 (155)	43 (136)	−9	45
Public law	37 (102)	43 (84)	−6	47

TABLE 5 (*continued*)

Issue	Success rate as petitioner (N)	When respondent, opponents' success rate (N)	Net advantage	Averaged success rate (as petitioner and respondent)
Average				
Civil rights and liberties	39 (7)	62 (9)	−13	44
Private economic	40 (319)	46 (267)	−6	47
Torts	34 (86)	54 (79)	−20	40
Public law	35 (203)	48 (131)	−13	43

though in forty-two public law cases associations were the petitioner and in twenty-seven public law cases they were the respondents before the Australian High Court. Associations are much less likely to bring challenges in South Africa. In public law disputes, associations enjoy a positive net advantage only in South Africa, where they also enjoy an averaged success rate as petitioner and respondent of 62 percent. Conversely, associations have a negative net advantage in all other countries, with a −36 percent net advantage in the UK and a −31 percent net advantage in India.

When they are involved in challenges to government regulation or government action, associations have the greatest success in civil rights and liberties cases, ranging from a net advantage of 67 percent in the Philippines, with only four such challenges, to 50 percent in the UK (only five challenges). Either groups elect not to pursue litigation as a strategy in these countries or they do so very sparingly. However, they fare better than their counterparts in South Africa (18 percent net advantage in a country not known for rights and liberties protections), Australia, India, or Canada. Associations are involved in few tort cases across our six courts but among those disputes, they achieve an averaged success rate of 55 percent and an averaged net advantage of 11 percent.

According to party capability theory, the government is the ultimate repeat player (Kritzer 2003; Kritzer and Silbey 2003), and as such, the government should enjoy the greatest advantage, and the most consistent advantage, across our six countries and across all issues. Table 7 presents evidence to the contrary. Even in criminal cases the government does not enjoy a consistent positive net advantage. In fact, the government has a negative net advantage in both Australia and South Africa, and while the government experiences positive net advantages in the other countries, only in Canada and the UK does the advantage appear substantial.

TABLE 6. Net advantage for association by issue (%)

Issue	Success rate as petitioner (N)	When respondent, opponents' success rate (N)	Net advantage	Averaged success rate (as petitioner and respondent)
Australia				
Civil rights and liberties	60 (5)	50 (2)	10	55
Private economic	41 (22)	64 (25)	−23	38
Torts		100 (1)		
Public law	31 (42)	37 (27)	−6	47
United Kingdom				
Civil rights and liberties	75 (4)	25 (1)	50	75
Private economic	67 (12)	36 (11)	30	65
Torts	40 (5)	75 (4)	−35	33
Public law	27 (11)	64 (11)	−36	32
Canada				
Civil rights and liberties	32 (19)	31 (13)	1	50
Private economic	31 (29)	50 (30)	−19	41
Torts	63 (8)	0 (4)	63	81
Public law	40 (53)	55 (29)	−16	42
India				
Civil rights and liberties	9 (11)	0 (0)	9	55
Private economic	61 (28)	32 (2)5	29	64
Torts	0 (3)		0	50
Public law	25 (85)	55 (29)	−31	35
Philippines				
Civil rights and liberties	67 (3)	0 (1)	67	83
Private economic	23 (57)	27 (30)	−4	48
Torts	33 (3)		33	67
Public law	36 (31)	47 (15)	−11	44
South Africa				
Civil rights and liberties	100 (1)	82 (11)	18	59
Private economic	34 (32)	41 (27)	−6	47
Torts	25 (4)	33 (3)	−8	46
Public law	53 (15)	29 (7)	25	62

TABLE 6 (*continued*)

Issue	Success rate as petitioner (N)	When respondent, opponents' success rate (N)	Net advantage	Averaged success rate (as petitioner and respondent)
Average				
Civil rights and liberties	57 (10)	38 (6)	26	63
Private economic	43 (36)	42 (30)	1	51
Torts	32 (6)	52 (3)	11	55
Public law	35 (61)	47 (27)	−12	44

In addition, the government has significant variation in its success rates in private economic cases. In the UK the government enjoys one of the highest net advantages of any petitioner or respondent across any issue category, 71 percent, but the government has a negative net advantage in private economic cases in the Philippines. While the government is not often involved in cases involving private economic disputes, some such challenges emerge across the countries. Most of these cases arise in disputes involving copyright infringement or patent disputes in which the government becomes a party. These issues are coded as private economic disputes. It is also the case that some parastatal entities will fall into this category. For example, in South Africa the Land Bank is a government-controlled private lending institution involved in agribusiness and insurance to promote economic growth. In a number of cases the Land Bank was sued or sued individuals or businesses in challenges involving contract or creditor issues. These cases are coded as private economic rather than public law.

When there are injury claims involving the government, the variation in the results repeats itself. The government has a negative net advantage of −45 percent in Australia, −18 percent in the UK, and −9 percent in South Africa. In each of these countries the government's averaged success rate ranges from only 28 percent in Australia to 46 percent in South Africa and 41 percent in the UK. Governments fare much better before their high courts in the Philippines, with an averaged success rate of 75 percent, and India, with an averaged success rate of 81 percent.

For public law challenges, the issue category with the largest number of cases, governments still do not fare consistently well, but certainly have greater success, with a positive net advantage in five of the six countries. While the averaged success rate of 54 percent across all six countries suggests

TABLE 7. Net advantage for government by issue (%)

Issue	Success rate as petitioner (N)	When respondent, opponents' success rate (N)	Net advantage	Averaged success rate (as petitioner and respondent)
Australia				
Criminal	40 (35)	52 (270)	−12	44
Civil rights and liberties	0 (2)	25 (12)	−25	38
Private economic	71 (7)	46 (11)	26	63
Torts	25 (4)	70 (10)	−45	28
Public law	61 (90)	44 (211)	18	59
United Kingdom				
Criminal	59 (70)	33 (166)	26	63
Civil rights and liberties	56 (9)	50 (28)	6	53
Private economic	100 (1)	29 (7)	71	86
Torts	27 (11)	46 (11)	−18	41
Public law	60 (109)	31 (140)	29	64
Canada				
Criminal	60 (45)	19 (120)	41	70
Civil rights and liberties	47 (19)	40 (50)	7	54
Private economic	60 (3)	43 (7)	17	59
Torts	50 (8	44 (9)	6	53
Public law	53 (102)	38 (227)	15	58
India				
Criminal	52 (67)	42 (336)	11	55
Civil rights and liberties	33 (3)	29 (35)	5	52
Private economic	63 (8)	41 (17)	21	61
Torts	100 (1)	39 (13)	62	81
Public law	47 (138)	33 (284)	14	57
Philippines				
Criminal	35 (46)	31 (182)	4	52
Civil rights and liberties	63 (8)	39 (26)	24	62
Private economic	16 (37)	44 (25)	−28	36
Torts	50 (2)	0 (3)	50	75
Public law	28 (126)	54 (167)	−26	37

TABLE 7 (*continued*)

Issue	Success rate as petitioner (N)	When respondent, opponents' success rate (N)	Net advantage	Averaged success rate (as petitioner and respondent)
South Africa				
Criminal	40 (35)	41 (389	−1	50
Civil rights and liberties	48 (25)	27 (11	21	60
Private economic	47 (15)	29 (24	18	59
Torts	38 (40)	46 (28	−9	46
Public law	40 (119)	38 (130	2	51
Average				
Criminal	48 (66)	36 (330)	11	56
Civil rights and liberties	42 (12)	34 (37)	8	54
Private economic	60 (13)	39 (20)	21	60
Torts	48 (11)	39 (16)	9	55
Public law	48 (146)	39 (262)	9	54

that governments in general do better than their challengers or those they challenge, there is significant variation in that success, ranging from a high of 64 percent averaged success rate in the UK to a low of 37 percent in the Philippines.

Discussion

Galanter's thesis accurately predicts the success of repeat players like Canary Wharf Ltd. and the Home Assurance Company when challenged by one-shotters like Patricia and Andrew. Focusing only on prototypical litigants as exemplified by these two cases can be misleading, however. Indeed, the findings of this analysis raise questions about the underlying stability of Galanter's classic argument, namely, that those presumed to have greater resources are most likely to succeed. Galanter's thesis has been a mainstay of the public law literature since its introduction to the discipline in 1974. Our findings are significant for several reasons, but most importantly because they emphasize the need to expand our theories beyond the boundaries of the US in particular and stable, industrialized democracies more generally. One might have presumed that Galanter's arguments concerning resources and outcomes would have been even more pronounced for developing countries, where resources are more unevenly distributed. In fact, our results suggest a more complex pattern.

Even after controlling for national differences and issues in the cases, there is some support for the key propositions of party capability theory as explicated by Galanter and others. However, overall the magnitude of that support is rather modest. The most notable findings consistent with Galanter's thesis are that governments, on average, tend to be more successful across the range of the countries we studied than other parties. In contrast, the expectation derived from party capability theory that corporations should be more successful than individuals does not hold across nations. The overall picture derived from these six countries is that businesses on average are less successful than individuals. Perhaps more important, the relative chance of success of individuals versus businesses varies substantially across nations and across issues. Our results also suggest that while Galanter's thesis may provide some insight, it is too simplistic to explain litigation outcomes for the highest courts of appeal across multiple nations and multiple issue categories.

It is also evident that more analysis is necessary to understand what is driving the variation across the nations included in this analysis. These countries differ on numerous social, political, and economic dimensions. Litigant resources may not be the best explanation for the variation among the parties. The relationship between the government and the courts could be an important factor. The insights of strategic accounts suggest that in authoritarian regimes, courts should anticipate the potential for sanctions from the government if they act contrary to government preferences and thus should provide authoritarian regimes with very high rates of success in court, at least until their demise is apparent (Helmke 2003, 2005). Haynie (1994, 1995) suggests that courts that lack institutional legitimacy may actually rule against the haves to increase their support among the population at large. These concerns may be magnified by variations in economic development.

Variations in the success rates of individuals and governments may also be a function of the types of constitutional guarantees articulated and the level of democratic governance. It may be that greater articulation of rights and liberties increases the likelihood of success for individuals (Camp Keith 2002; Camp Keith, Tate, and Poe 2009), though our results suggest a more complicated explanation.

Judicial ideology may also play a role. Research on the US Supreme Court suggests that judges are motivated by personal policy preferences (Segal 1984; Segal and Cover 1989; Segal and Spaeth 1996a, 1996b, 2002). The effects of ideology may vary across countries and across issues.

In addition, differences among the courts in terms of jurisdiction, nature of issues, extent of judicial review, degree of sponsorship, interest group activity, and any number of other structural and contextual factors can have an impact on the extent to which litigant resources influence judicial outcomes. The cross-national perspective of our research allows us to develop more rigorous, complex, and truly generalizable theories concerning courts, litigation, and outcomes. In chapter 4 we explore more critically the success of the government across our countries, evaluating both national and subnational levels of government.

4 | Examining the Success of the Government Gorilla

MR. MOORTHY, A resident of Krishnarajanagara in the southern Indian state of Karnataka, found himself at the center of a rather mundane and yet interesting conundrum for the state.[1] Quite the entrepreneur, Mr. Moorthy had rather ingeniously engineered a system to tap the government's electricity grid without registering any use on his meter. Unfortunately for Mr. Moorthy, a routine inspection one morning by Syed Ameer, a supervisor for the Karnataka Electricity Board, uncovered the ruse. He returned with an assistant engineer and the junior engineer later that afternoon and gathered the evidence of the theft of electricity, a criminal offense under sections 39 and 44 of the Electricity Act of 1910. At the direction of the assistant engineer, Mr. Ameer submitted a report to the police, who investigated the complaint and issued a challan, the equivalent of a citation. On July 10, 1979, Mr. Moorthy appeared before the lower court judge, or munsiff and judicial magistrate first class. In his reading of the facts and the law, the magistrate was troubled by section 50 of the Electricity Act, which he felt did not convey to a supervisor like Mr. Ameer the authority to lodge the complaint. The statute prohibited any prosecution "except at the instance of the Government or an Electrical Inspector,"[2] and since Mr. Ameer was neither, Mr. Moorthy must be, and was, acquitted, despite sufficient evidence of his guilt. In most cases like Mr. Moorthy's, the state would have ended its prosecution, but as Kritzer notes, the state can pick and choose, and in this case it utilized its authority to appeal the acquittal. In the High Court, the prosecution hung its hat on the phrase "at the instance." Surely, the prosecutors argued, Mr. Ameer had lodged the complaint "at the instance" or direction of the appropriate electrical engineer, thereby satisfying both the letter and spirit of the law. Moreover, the state argued, the Karnataka Electricity Board had issued a notification specifically authorizing junior engineers, section officers, and supervisors (like Mr. Ameer), to lodge complaints.[3] The Karnataka High Court reviewed the plain meaning of the words of section 50 and held firm to the acquittal.[4] The court also rejected the notification as insufficient to overcome the requirements of section 50 because it had not been published in the official government's *Gazette*.[5]

The state's last resort was the Supreme Court of India, and it chose to appeal the lower court's interpretation of the statute, as well as the court's rejection of the expansion of individuals authorized to bring complaints. Thus Mr. Moorthy, now having secured two advocates to argue his case, found himself before the highest court of the land for the equivalent of a traffic citation. But the state's goal, as Galanter argues it often is, was the long game. In fact, the state conceded that it was only interested in the point of law at issue and was not interested in the imposition of any punishment for Mr. Moorthy. It was especially concerned about the lower court's narrow interpretation of the phrase "at the instance of." The state argued that the engineer, or a similarly situated public servant, could meet the requirement of the law by urging or entreating others on their behalf to bring the charges—others like Mr. Ameer. While the rupees lost to Mr. Moorthy's entrepreneurship were of less concern to the state, broadening the interpretation of who has authority to lodge complaints across a broad spectrum of offenses named in a variety of statutes was of concern.

The Supreme Court, as Galanter predicts, favored the state. It cited appropriate past precedents,[6] including one from the Karnataka High Court itself,[7] and turned to the *Random House Dictionary of the English Language* to determine the meaning of "at the instance of." In the end, the court found that the narrow reading of section 50's dictate was "wholly unwarranted" and "resulted in manifest miscarriage of justice."[8] The Supreme Court also rejected the lower court's requirement of publication in the *Gazette*.[9] The state established broader authority for governing bodies such as the Karnataka Electricity Board and preserved its ability to combat theft. After three court judgments, all of which agreed there was sufficient evidence for a conviction of theft, Mr. Moorthy faced no penalty.

While India's Supreme Court behaved as Galanter would predict, research suggests that the have-nots can gain access to the resources identified by Galanter that can potentially level the playing field—resources such as talented and skilled lawyers, articulated rights and liberties, and ideologically sympathetic judges, any one of which might tip the balance of the scales that normally enjoy the thumb of the government gorilla.

Such was the case of Augustina Garfin Panotes, who taught for more than thirty years for the Filipino Ministry of Education and Culture. Her last assignment was with the Francisco Balagtas Elementary School in Manila. In October 1979 Augustina was admitted to the hospital with severe abdominal pain and vomiting, and was ultimately diagnosed with colon cancer. Two operations failed to save her life and on May 23, 1980, seven months after her initial diagnosis, she died at the age of fifty. Her husband, Venusto, applied for compensation from the government, arguing that her employment as an elementary schoolteacher had increased the risk of her developing cancer. Among other things, he argued that the nature of her work, meetings, and school activities required her to skip meals or to take her meals at irregular times, leaving her weak and susceptible to the disease and exacerbating the "gastric influence" that predisposed her to cancer. Moreover, he argued, because of her employment, her disease worsened, resulting in her "early demise." The Government Service Insurance System (GSIS) denied the claim on the grounds that the "supposition" that his wife's irregular meals in the course of her employment gave rise to her "ailment" lacked a "medical basis." The GSIS further argued that there was no evidence that Augustina had ever been exposed to toxic chemicals or radioactive substances in any of her thirty years of employment with the ministry.[10] While the exact cause of colon cancer remains elusive, even in 1980 the consumption of meals on an irregular basis or skipping them entirely was not considered a risk factor for cancer of any type, including the colon cancer that took the life of Venusto's wife.

Mr. Panotes pressed his petition to then president Marcos in a letter dated February 12, 1982. Fortunately for Mr. Panotes, the letter technically was considered an appeal to the Employees' Compensation Commission, the body that reviews the decisions of the GSIS. Venusto argued that while it was true that colon cancer was not an occupational disease for elementary schoolteachers, the working conditions increased the risk that such cancer could develop.

Mr. Panotes lost in his appeal to the GSIS but found a more sympathetic ear with the Philippine Supreme Court, to which he appealed his loss. The court ruled that the plaintiff only needed to demonstrate a "reasonable work-connection" rather than "actual proof."[11] The court then determined that such a reasonable connection was evident insofar as the cause of colon cancer, at least at the time and in Augustina's case, was unknown, and surely the constant "physical, mental and emotional pressure" she faced in her position "was of course very detrimental to her health," especially in light of the "unhygienic" classrooms of Filipino elementary schools.[12] In the "natural course" of her work as a classroom teacher, Augustina would have been assigned to other "far and dirty places where she could have contracted viruses and parasites." Moreover, the court reasoned, "her constant exposure to chalk and dust, to the vagaries of nature when attending school activities," would have taken a natural toll on her health.[13] These factors, in addition to the missed meals, argued the court, "likely" weakened her body and resulted in the cancerous invasion that took her life. The court concluded that when the cause of the cancer is not definitive, and it rarely is, the right to compensation must be "liberally construed."[14] Ultimately Mr. Panotes was compensated 12,000 pesos, about $670 at the time.

The court's empathy for employees can be found in numerous decisions that distributed resources to those with less (Tate and Haynie 1994; Haynie 1994, 1995). Indeed, Justice Hugo E. Gutierrez complained in his dissent in Mr. Panotes's appeal that the court was "enacting its own employment compensation law, contrary to the existing law passed by the proper lawmaking authority," when the court determined "that any and all causes of death or disability are valid grounds for the payment of employees' compensation benefits."[15] Such empathy serves as a significant advantage for have-nots like Augustina and Venusto Panotes when challenging the haves like the Employees' Compensation Commission, the GSIS, and the Ministry of Education and Culture, all components of the government gorilla.

The cases of Mr. Moorthy and Mr. Panotes are interesting examples of the conflicts that arise in the highest courts of appeal across the globe. Unlike with the US Supreme Court, where such fact-based disputes would almost never make it onto the docket, such appeals arise far more routinely in other countries. Moreover, their resolution is considered critical to the rule of law. The more expansive nature of the docket can also lead to larger numbers of disputes in these countries. The Indian and the Philippine Supreme Courts hear over a thousand disputes annually, many mired in contestations of fact or statutory interpretation. These courts also hear incredibly important challenges affecting public policy more broadly, but for Mr. Moorthy and Mr. Panotes, the ability to pursue their appeal is critical to the respect for the rule of law in their countries. Even more critical is the fact that their highest courts of appeal entertain such challenges of the regime.

In the previous chapter we explored Galanter's thesis broadly across the dockets, the litigant combinations, and the case outcomes of our sample six countries and found substantial variation. In this chapter we focus on one particular "upperdog" that has garnered substantial scholarly attention, the government. As Galanter notes, the government is especially privileged in the legal system. The government is the ultimate repeat player, with experienced legal talent that can shape the rules and bend them to favorable interpretation. The government can scan the universe of cases before it and sift for those most advantageous to its long-term interests. The government staffs the courts and can leverage the informal and ongoing relationships with the institutional incumbents, while one-shotters like Mr. Moorthy and Mr. Panotes move into and through the system in a singular instance. The government also has the ability to bring substantial resources to bear in the navigation of time-consuming and resource-intensive litigation. Moreover, as Galanter notes, the rules favor the powerful, and the government reflects and protects those interests.

Kritzer argues that the government has an overwhelming advantage relative to other litigants. Indeed, he asserts that the "government gorilla" is especially advantaged in appellate courts, the venue for our study (Kritzer 2003). As we noted in chapter 1, Kritzer argues that the government creates the rules the courts enforce, which provides a distinct advantage, and those rules are enforced by judges who are themselves government officials. Across the dockets of our six countries, criminal cases represent the largest issue category. We expect to find significant advantages for the government in these cases. The government determines whom to charge, what to charge, and whom to try or plea, and the government can bring experience, expertise, and theoretically endless resources to the appellate process should the prosecution be challenged. In the six countries we study, the criminal cases range from the mundane to murder and almost everything in between.

The analyses in chapter 4 demonstrate that the government does not fare consistently well across all six countries and across all issue categories. In this chapter we explore potential reasons for the variation in the results evidenced in the analyses of winners and losers in courts of law. We first explore the potential for differences in litigation outcomes based on the level of government involved. We explore who wins and who loses, comparing national to subnational governments. Our data allow us to explore the possibility that the national government conforms to the expectations of party capability theory, while subnational governments do not enjoy the advantages generally credited to Kritzer's government gorilla. First, the significant resources available to the national government are surely less at the subnational level. In each of our countries the taxing and revenue powers of the state and provincial governments are less than those of the national government. In terms of utilizing strategies to "play for the rules," the national government should have greater ability to selectively sift through its options and should have more resources, that is, more money, legal talent, experience, and expertise, which should allow it to succeed more often than subnational governments.

Second, the decisions of these courts are the responsibility of judges serving at the national level. All the courts in our study function under unified judiciaries. That is, while there are lower-level courts, they are all units of a single judiciary; there are no separate provincial or state court systems. As a result, only the national government is responsible for appointing judges. The influence of subnational governments on appointments to the state or provincial courts whose work is overseen by the appellate courts of our study is functional, not structural. Since the national government officially appoints the judges of our courts, we would expect greater deference to national than to subnational governments.

Third, the national government controls the sandbox. The actions of the subnational governments must conform to the rules created by the national government. National governments are unlikely to endure behavior from subnational governments that could threaten their dominance. Behavior by subnational governments that alters or attempts to circumvent the power of the national government in social control and conflict resolution is unlikely to be tolerated. The national government can rewrite the rules or establish new rules to ensure its authority.

Ultimately, both national and subnational governments are repeat players. They should reap the benefits of that status. The analyses in chapter 3 suggest that there is significant variation across different legal systems. Analyzing national and subnational government success should provide greater insight into why this variation exists. To that end, we replicate the analyses of the prior chapter, but we disaggregate the national and subnational governments. Table 8 shows the net advantage of petitioners and respondents across our six countries. In each of these countries, the national government has both the greater net advantage and higher averaged success rates. The differences are minimal for Canada, the UK, and India but larger for Australia, South Africa, and the Philippines. Only the subnational governments of South Africa and Australia have negative net advantages among the six countries. The subnational governments of these two countries also have an averaged success rate below 50 percent. In the Philippines the national government enjoys a net advantage of 18 against its challengers, but the provincial governments retain only a net advantage of 2. This pattern persists in Australia and South Africa. The national governments of the UK and Canada enjoy higher averaged success rates, at 62 percent and 61 percent, respectively, while the subnational governments of South Africa (48 percent) and Australia (47 percent) have the lowest averaged success rates.

TABLE 8. Net advantage of national and subnational governments before the high courts, 1970–2000 (%)

Level of government	Success rate as petitioner	When respondent, opponent's success rate	Net advantage	Averaged success rate (as petitioner and respondent)
Australia				
National	55	48	7	53
Subnational	48	53	−5	47
Canada				
National	54	33	22	61
Subnational	55	35	20	60
United Kingdom				
National	57	33	24	62
Subnational	54	37	17	58
India				
National	50	37	13	57
Subnational	50	38	12	56
Philippines				
National	46	28	18	59
Subnational	39	37	2	51
South Africa				
National	41	40	2	51
Subnational	38	43	−5	48
Average				
National	51	36	14	57
Subnational	47	41	7	53

While the previous results focus on the overall success rates of national and subnational governments, we further analyze government success when governments challenge individuals, corporations, associations, or each other. Table 9 presents the results for government success against different respondents. Again, there is substantial variation across the countries studied. The national government is least likely to succeed when challenging individuals in Australia (46 percent) and South Africa (43 percent). It has the highest rate of

TABLE 9. National and subnational government success rates against different respondents before high courts, 1970–2000 (%)

Level of government	Respondent (N)				
	Individual	Corporation	Association	National government	Subnational government
Australia					
National	46 (74)	63 (52)	100 (1)		63 (8)
Subnational	61 (66)	41 (44)	33 (15)	41 (22)	
Canada					
National	52 (98)	58 (60)	83 (6)		57 (14)
Subnational	58 (327)	48 (69)	44 (18)	13 (8)	
United Kingdom					
National	59 (117)	49 (63)	71 (7)		78 (9)
Subnational	59 (88)	49 (35)	50 (4)	22 (9)	
India					
National	52 (150)	44 (55)	75 (8)		67 (3)
Subnational	56 (236)	43 (147)	45 (11)	33 (6)	
Philippines					
National	53 (162)	34 (38)	35 (17)		53 (15)
Subnational	37 (19)	67 (6)		33 (9)	
South Africa					
National	43 (120)	45 (80)	60 (10)		0 (3)
Subnational	32 (44)	52 (31)	67 (3)	0 (4)	
Average					
National	51 (120)	49 (58)	71 (8)		53 (9)
Subnational	51 (130)	50 (55)	48 (10)	24 (10)	

success when facing individuals in the UK (59 percent), and a slightly better than 50 percent success rate in Canada, India, and the Philippines.

The converse is true for subnational governments in Australia, with a substantially higher success rate against individuals, 61 percent, compared to that of the national government, 46 percent. This is also true in Canada and India, but subnational governments have lower success rates than the national government against individuals in the Philippines and South Africa. There is no difference in success rates between the national and subnational government in challenges involving individuals for the UK.

When the national government challenges corporations, it is most likely to succeed in Australia, whereas subnational governments are substantially less likely to succeed in Australia when facing corporations. Only in the Philippines and South Africa do the subnational governments fare better than the national government when challenging corporations. There is again no difference in the UK between success rates of the national and subnational governments involved in legal disputes with corporations. Across the high courts we study, associations are the least likely to face either the national or the subnational government and, with the exception of the Philippines, are much less likely to succeed against the national government when they do. It is also evident that when the national government and a subnational government face each other in the high courts we study, the national government is much more likely to succeed. Subnational governments have the lowest rate of success in South Africa, where they did not have any success against the government (though only four challenges reached the highest court of appeal). Success also evaded provincial governments in Canada when challenging the national government. Subnational governments had the highest success rates when challenging the national government in Australia but still did not succeed in even half the cases.

Next, we examine the net advantage for different combination of parties. Again, we note variation. Individuals have a positive net advantage when litigating against corporations in every country. The largest negative net advantages appear when individuals and the government are at bar, ranging from a −27 net advantage for individuals in the UK to −9 in the Philippines. Individuals also struggle against the government in Canada (−21) and India (−13). Only in Australia do individuals have a positive net advantage against the government. The results in table 10 echo the findings above: individuals fare better against corporations than Galanter would predict, and corporations struggle when challenging the government, in line with Galanter's prediction.

Table 11 focuses on the success rates of the government when defendants challenge aspects of criminal prosecutions. Here again we see variation. Challenges involving crimes of violence constitute the largest component of the criminal challenges with the exception of Canada, and the government enjoys the greatest net advantage in this issue area in Canada, the Philippines, and South Africa. The government has less success in challenges involving violent crimes in the UK and India, and the government has a remarkable −37 net

TABLE 10. Net advantage for different combinations of parties (%)

Parties	Net advantage
Australia	
Individual v. corporation	1
Individual v. government	5
Corporation v. government	−20
Canada	
Individual v. corporation	10
Individual v. government	−21
Corporation v. government	−17
United Kingdom	
Individual v. corporation	2
Individual v. government	−27
Corporation v. government	−17
India	
Individual v. corporation	14
Individual v. government	−13
Corporation v. government	−9
Philippines	
Individual v. corporation	19
Individual v. government	−9
Corporation v. government	−17
South Africa	
Individual v. corporation	3
Individual v. government	−3
Corporation v. government	−9
Average	
Individual v. corporation	8
Individual v. government	−11
Corporation v. government	−15

TABLE 11. Net advantage for government in criminal issues (%)

Issue	Success rate as petitioner (N)	When respondent, opponents' success rate (N)	Net advantage	Averaged success rate (as petitioner and respondent)
Australia				
Crimes of violence	19 (16)	56 (163)	−37	32
Property crimes	80 (5)	50 (38)	30	65
Drug and morality offenses	25 (4)	49 (37)	−24	38
Government corruption	100 (3)	33 (3)	67	84
Political crimes				
Other crimes	43 (7)	38 (29)	5	53
United Kingdom				
Crimes of violence	43 (21)	26 (69)	17	59
Property crimes	64 (22)	35 (34)	29	65
Drug and morality offenses	86 (7)	30 (20)	56	78
Government corruption				
Political crimes	100 (2)	25 (4)	75	88
Other crimes	56 (18)	46 (39)	10	55
Canada				
Crimes of violence	25 (4)	0 (2)	25	63
Property crimes		0 (5)		
Drug and morality offenses	64 (25)	18 (100)	46	73
Government corruption				
Political crimes				
Other crimes	63 (16)	38 (13)	25	63
India				
Crimes of violence	41 (29)	38 (196)	3	52
Property crimes	89 (9)	55 (31)	34	67
Drug and morality offenses	100 (1)	20 (10)	80	90
Government corruption	33 (6)	58 (19)	−25	38
Political crimes		33 (6)		
Other crimes	55 (22)	45 (74)	10	55
Philippines				
Crimes of violence	42 (12)	18 (553)	24	62
Property crimes	64 (14)	38 (58)	26	63
Drug and morality offenses	0 (1)	17 (63)	−17	42
Government corruption	75 (8)	42 (38)	33	67
Political crimes		50 (4)		
Other crimes	64 (11)	35 (23)	29	65

TABLE 11 (*continued*)

Issue	Success rate as petitioner (N)	When respondent, opponents' success rate (N)	Net advantage	Averaged success rate (as petitioner and respondent)
South Africa				
Crimes of violence	63 (8)	40 (219)	23	62
Property crimes	33 (6)	46 (48)	−13	44
Drug and morality offenses	20 (5)	52 (29)	−32	34
Government corruption		33 (3)		
Political crimes	40 (5)	50 (34)	−10	45
Other crimes	36 (11)	27 (56)	9	55
Average				
Crimes of violence	39 (15)	30 (200)	9	55
Property crimes	66 (11)	45 (42)	21	61
Drug and morality offenses	49 (7)	31 (43)	18	59
Government corruption	69 (6)	42 (16)	25	63
Political crimes	70 (4)	40 (12)	33	66
Other crimes	53 (14)	38 (39)	15	57

advantage in Australia, where the government averages success in about one-third of the cases. In all other countries the government enjoys a 50 percent or better averaged success rate. Thus, for cases involving the most serious crimes, the government on average enjoys a positive advantage.

With the exception of South Africa, the government enjoys an advantage in challenges involving property crimes, but in only three of the six countries— the UK, Canada, and India—does the government enjoy a positive net advantage in challenges involving drug and morality offenses. Challenges of government corruption and political crimes also show greater variation, with no challenges involving political crimes decided by the Canadian or Australian high courts and with cases involving issues of political crimes constituting the smallest component of the docket across all nations with the exception of South Africa. Given the criminal prosecutions under its oppressive apartheid regime, this is not surprising.

If there is any issue area where one would predict the government to prevail, it surely would be in criminal cases, where the government enjoys substantial control. While on average the government enjoys a positive net advantage in criminal cases, this finding is not universal across all countries and all crimes.

Table 12 presents the net advantage for the government in civil rights and liberties issues. What is striking is how little of the docket these cases take up in the courts we study. In several countries there are no cases in which individuals have challenged the government on voting or religious rights. Because of the small number of challenges, both averages and net advantage can be highly skewed. For example, in the UK the government as petitioner won 100 percent of cases involving equal treatment issues, but there were only two such cases. When the government was the respondent $(N = 7)$ on such issues, its opponents won 71 percent of the time. While the averaged success rate of the government in the UK for equal treatment cases is an impressive 65 percent, this should be tempered by the small number of such challenges. In India, the Philippines, and South Africa, very few cases fall into these categories. This is in contrast to the US, where civil rights and liberties account for a substantial portion of the court's docket. Docket composition is important across our high courts. Governments can consider it a victory if they are rarely before the high court in certain issue areas, especially potentially high-stakes issue areas such as rights and liberties. As Galanter argues, the government as the ultimate repeat player can select which cases to appeal and which to settle.

We see similar variation in who wins and who loses in cases in which appellants and respondents challenge government regulation across a number of issue areas. For example, across our countries, on average the government appears as petitioner in only two cases and as respondent in only three cases involving health and safety regulations. While the averaged success rate in challenges to the government's regulation of health and safety is an impressive 77 percent, it is clear that such challenges rarely reach the high courts in these six countries. Conversely, challenges to government taxation and to government benefits and employment occur more frequently across all the countries we study. In this more frequently litigated area, the government enjoys an advantage, with the exception of India. In India, the government is successful in only 27 percent of its taxation challenges but does better when challenged, for an averaged success rate of 43 percent. For challenges to the government's regulation of benefits and employment, the Philippine Supreme Court seems least receptive to the government's appeals: the government enjoys an averaged success rate of 33 percent. The government fares much better before the high courts of South Africa (72 percent averaged success rate) and the UK

TABLE 12. Net advantage for government in civil rights and liberties issues (%)

Issue	Success rate as petitioner (N)	When respondent, opponents' success rate (N)	Net advantage	Averaged success rate (as petitioner and respondent)
Australia				
Equal treatment		0 (2)	0	100
Voting rights				
Speech, press, assembly, petition		67 (3)	−67	33
Religious rights				
Rights of Indigenous peoples	0 (1)	0 (2)	0	50
Other rights	0 (2)	25 (4)	−25	38
United Kingdom				
Equal treatment	100 (2)	71 (7)	29	65
Voting rights				
Speech, press, assembly, petition		0 (2)	0	100
Religious rights				
Rights of Indigenous peoples				
Other rights				
Canada				
Equal treatment	100 (1)	38 (8)	62	81
Voting rights	50 (2)	100 (2)	−50	25
Speech, press, assembly, petition	33 (3)	44 (9)	−11	45
Religious rights		0 (4)	0	100
Rights of Indigenous peoples	33 (3)	0 (2)	33	67
Other rights	33 (6)	33 (6)	0	50
India				
Equal treatment		0 (2)	0	100
Voting rights		100 (1)	−100	0
Speech, press, assembly, petition		0 (4)	0	100
Religious rights		0 (1)	0	100
Rights of Indigenous peoples				
Other rights				

Issue	Success rate as petitioner (N)	When respondent, opponents' success rate (N)	Net advantage	Averaged success rate (as petitioner and respondent)
Philippines				
Equal treatment	0 (1)		0	50
Voting rights				
Speech, press, assembly, petition		60 (5)	−60	40
Religious rights				
Rights of Indigenous peoples				
Other rights				
South Africa				
Equal treatment				
Voting rights				
Speech, press, assembly, petition	63 (8)	0 (2)	63	82
Religious rights				
Rights of Indigenous peoples				
Other rights				
Average				
Equal treatment	67 (1)	27 (5)	39	70
Voting rights	50 (2)	100 (2)	−50	25
Speech, press, assembly, petition	48 (6)	29 (4)	20	60
Religious rights		0 (3)	0	100
Rights of Indigenous peoples	17 (2)	0 (2)	17	58
Other rights	17 (4)	29 (5)	−13	44

(77 percent averaged success rate) in challenges to government benefits and employment issues. Governments fare much better on immigration challenges, with averaged success rates ranging from 53 percent (Australia) to 83 percent (Canada), though very few cases challenging immigration regulation come before the courts of South Africa or India.

We do not find a government gorilla consistently emerging from our analysis. Our results suggest that the government enjoys the dominance that

TABLE 13. Net advantage for government in public law issues (%)

Issue	Success rate as petitioner (N)	When respondent, opponents' success rate (N)	Net advantage	Averaged success rate (as petitioner and respondent)
Australia				
Health and safety regulation	100 (1)	50 (2)	50	75
Environmental regulation	75 (4)	33 (3)	42	71
Agriculture and land use regulation	50 (4)	50 (2)	0	50
Government regulation of labor		34 (29)		
Taxation	57 (51)	46 (110)	11	56
Government benefits and employment	75 (4)	71 (7)	4	52
Immigration and citizenship	54 (13)	48 (21)	6	53
Other public law	77 (13)	35 (37)	42	71
United Kingdom				
Health and safety regulation	100 (2)	0 (1)	100	100
Environmental regulation	0 (1)	40 (5)	−40	30
Agriculture and land use regulation	67 (3)	18 (11)	49	75
Government regulation of labor	60 (5)			
Taxation	55 (58)	39 (62)	16	58
Government benefits and employment	78 (9)	25 (16)	53	77
Immigration and citizenship	67 (9)	24 (21)	43	72
Other public law	59 (22)	25 (24)	34	67
Canada				
Health and safety regulation	0 (1)	33 (3)	−33	34
Environmental regulation	80 (5)	50 (10)	30	65
Agriculture and land use regulation	57 (7)	50 (16)	7	54
Government regulation of labor	67 (3)	25 (8)	42	71
Taxation	45 (42)	36 (76)	9	55
Government benefits and employment	54 (13)	53 (30)	1	51
Immigration and citizenship	100 (5)	35 (34)	65	83
Other public law	50 (26)	30 (50)	20	60

Issue	Success rate as petitioner (N)	When respondent, opponents' success rate (N)	Net advantage	Averaged success rate (as petitioner and respondent)
India				
Health and safety regulation	100 (1)	25 (8)	75	88
Environmental regulation	100 (2)	17 (18)	83	92
Agriculture and land use regulation	71 (7)	21 (24)	50	75
Government regulation of labor	17 (6)	0 (3)	17	59
Taxation	27 (45)	42 (67)	−15	43
Government benefits and Employment	58 (64)	40 (116)	18	59
Immigration and citizenship		0 (1)	0	100
Other public law	54 (13)	19 (47)	35	68
Philippines				
Health and safety regulation	100 (1)			
Environmental regulation				
Agriculture and land use regulation	53 (30)	37 (19)	16	58
Government regulation of labor	0 (1)	33 (9)	−33	34
Taxation	50 (22)	14 (28)	36	68
Government benefits and employment	35 (26)	69 (127)	−34	33
Immigration and citizenship	63 (16)	39 (18)	24	62
Other public law	47 (32)	34 (62)	13	57
South Africa				
Health and safety regulation	50 (4)	0 (1)	50	75
Environmental regulation		0 (2)		
Agriculture and land use regulation	50 (8)	45 (11)	5	53
Government regulation of labor		100 (1)		
Taxation	39 (76)	38 (74)	1	51
Government benefits and employment	63 (8)	20 (5)	43	72
Immigration and citizenship		50 (2)		
Other public law	26 (23)	38 (34)	−12	44

TABLE 13 (*continued*)

Issue	Success rate as petitioner (N)	When respondent, opponents' success rate (N)	Net advantage	Averaged success rate (as petitioner and respondent)
Average				
Health and safety regulation	75 (2)	22 (3)	53	77
Environmental regulation	64 (3)	28 (8)	36	68
Agriculture and land use regulation	58 (10)	37 (14)	21	61
Government regulation of labor	36 (4)	38 (10)	−2	49
Taxation	46 (49)	36 (70)	10	55
Government benefits and employment	61 (21)	46 (50)	14	57
Immigration and citizenship	71 (11)	33 (16)	38	69
Other public law	52 (22)	30 (42)	22	61

Galanter predicts in some issue areas and in some countries, but not over-whelmingly or dependably so. Our results demonstrate that there is substantial variation across the countries we study in who wins and who loses. Mr. Panotes challenged the government in an issue area that clearly had the sympathy of the Philippine Supreme Court. Challengers enjoyed a two in three chance of success, and despite the long odds of demonstrating the link between cancer and the teaching profession, he prevailed. Mr. Moorthy won by losing before the Indian Supreme Court. He faced no punishment, but the Indian government achieved the interpretation of the statute it desired. Why did the government fail in its desired interpretation of the law in Mr. Panotes's case but succeed in Mr. Moorthy's challenge? We explore that variation further in chapter 5.

5 | A Comparative Analysis of Party Capability Theory

THOUSANDS OF INDIVIDUALS were ensnared in the crisis-fueled state that was South Africa in the 1980s. In the last week of October 1985, Mohammed Dullah Omar joined tens of thousands of detainees imprisoned under a series of states of emergency declared by President P. W. Botha.[1] Mr. Omar faced a daunting legal challenge in his fight for his freedom. The bureaucracy required to preserve apartheid was as vast as it was oppressive. At the center of that bureaucracy were courts and the judges who staffed them. Interpreting the various statutes and ordinances was essential to maintaining a semblance of law and order, and order was declining precipitously in the waning years of apartheid. Thousands died in township uprisings, the number of strikes rose dramatically, violence from the political opposition reached new levels, and government services, including education, were crumbling under the weight of the unrest.[2] The state brought its impressive arsenal of security statutes to combat the crisis, which was quickly spiraling out of control. Mr. Omar's petition ultimately landed before the Appellate Division (now the Supreme Court of Appeal), the highest court in apartheid South Africa.

Mr. Omar had become entangled in one of the many internal security statutes passed by parliament. While every country in our study has laws to protect the security interests of the state, for South Africa the threat was not from a minority group motivated by perceived or real grievances but from the majority Black population intent on toppling an authoritarian regime that preserved power, privilege, and property for whites. These laws, adopted in a system with parliamentary supremacy, restricted every aspect of the lives of Black South Africans, including their ability to move freely or own property, to love, to marry freely, to speak freely, and to associate and assemble freely.[3] The freedom to associate and assemble was seen as especially threatening to the apartheid regime, which strengthened its grip on the political opposition through a series of increasingly despotic statutes, including the Public Safety Act of 1953,[4] the Criminal Law Amendment Act (Act No. 8 of 1953),[5] the Internal Security Act (Act No. 74 of 1982), the Suppression of Communism Act of 1950,[6] the Riotous Assemblies Act of 1956,[7] the Unlawful Organizations

Act (Act No. 34 of 1960),[8] the Sabotage Act of 1962,[9] the ninety-day Detention Law of 1962,[10] the 180-Day Detention Law of 1963,[11] the Terrorism Act of 1967,[12] the Prohibition of Political Interference Act of 1968,[13] and the Internal Security Act of 1982,[14] among others.

Despite this impressive and repressive arsenal and the military and paramilitary used to enforce it, violence and unrest escalated as the minority National Party began its precipitous and fatal decline in the mid-1980s. Ultimately, President Botha declared a state of emergency on July 21, 1985, for certain areas, providing unfettered power to the executive branch. As unrest continued to spread throughout the country, the president extended the state of emergency to the whole nation on June 12, 1986.

Abdullah Mohamed Omar, the appellant in our case, came to the attention of the state president for the egregious error of serving as an attorney for those ensnared in apartheid's labyrinth of sanctions, and more critically for supporting the United Democratic Front (UDF), a political movement committed to abolishing segregation and the institutional and systemic racism that sustained it.[15] But Mr. Omar was on the radar of the regime long before December 1986.

Mr. Omar was born in Observatory, Cape Town, to immigrant parents from India. He graduated with a law degree from the University of Cape Town in 1957 and became a highly respected and successful advocate in the city, though annual permission had to be granted under the Group Areas Act for him to remain and practice there.[16] He became the official attorney for the Pan-African Congress, representing a number of accused in political trials. He represented both the South African Students' Organization and the Black People's Convention, and began to support the UDF in the 1980s.[17] The last affiliation almost certainly would have caught the attention of the regime. After all, merely advocating on behalf of any of these organizations would have run afoul of any number of security regulations.[18] The state had a cornucopia of options available to it in its quest to silence and sanction Mr. Omar. It chose instead to rely on President Botha's state of emergency order imposed via Proclamation R120 of 1985 as authorized by section 2 (1) of the Public Safety Act of 1953. This option was among the most oppressive.

Mr. Omar had little reason to suspect he would be successful before the court. In a series of decisions, the Appellate Division had rarely challenged the executive in critical cases (Cameron 1982). Indeed, the high court had overturned lower court decisions that had sought to provide some protection against the harshest of state sanctions.[19] The Appellate Division had earned the reputation of being "executive minded," especially under acting chief justice Rabie, who led the panel deciding Mr. Omar's case and would author the opinion that determined his fate.[20]

But Mr. Omar did have Arthur Chaskalson as his advocate. Mr. Chaskalson was a renowned member of the bar who had challenged the apartheid legal order his entire career. Most famously, in the 1963–64 Rivonia trial he had represented Nelson Mandela, Walter Sisulu, Thabo Mbeki, and five others charged with sabotage, a crime punishable by death. While all were found guilty, they were spared the death penalty the government had sought, a remarkable feat on the part of the defense lawyers. Advocate Chaskalson established the Legal Resources Centre in 1979 and, under its aegis, fought against apartheid's abuses, with success in a number of important cases.[21] He was a graduate of the University of Witwatersrand School of Law, one of the country's elite legal programs, and had navigated the South African legal system for almost thirty years by the time of Mr. Omar's detention. His co-counsel was Jeremy Gauntlet, already a well-regarded figure in the South African legal system. Chaskalson also represented two additional detainees before the court, and his co-counsel for those two cases, heard alongside Mr. Omar's, was Gilbert Marcus. Advocate Marcus, a rising star, would emerge as a national leader on a variety of rights and liberties issues. Mr. Omar could not have acquired greater legal talent, one of the key resources Galanter identifies.

Second, the lower court decision was a divided one, at least on one of the critical issues. In addition, the case was heard with two others, *Fani and Others v. Minister of Law and Order and Others*[22] and *Bill v. State President and Others*.[23] In the former, the lower court had ruled in favor of the detainees and had ordered their release. In the latter, the lower court ruled that the minister of law and order had to provide in writing the reason for the extended detention and had to allow the detainee to consult with counsel. The judges of the lower courts provided the appellate court with blueprints for have-not rulings.

Advocate Chaskalson, on behalf of Mr. Omar, challenged the detention in two respects. First, he argued that regulation 3 (3) of the president's order was ultra vires, or beyond the powers afforded him under the enabling legislation, namely, the Public Safety Act. This regulation reads: "3 (3) The Minister may, without notice to any person and without hearing any person, by written notice signed by him and addressed to the head of a prison, order that any person arrested and detained in terms of subreg (1), be further detained in that prison for the period mentioned in the notice."

Second, Advocate Chaskalson argued that regulation 3 (10) (a) was similarly ultra vires. This section provided that no person other than the minister or a person acting by virtue of his office "shall have access to any person detained in terms of the provisions of this regulation, except with the consent of and subject to such conditions as may be determined by the Minister or the Commissioner of the South African Police."

Under the order, Mr. Omar was arrested and his detention was extended.[24] This extension, Advocate Chaskalson argued, required the government to allow Mr. Omar (1) to present a defense and (2) access to a legal adviser, protections clearly not sanctioned under the state of emergency. These two issues were brought before the Cape Provincial Decision.[25]

Basic fairness, Advocate Chaskalson reasoned, demanded Mr. Omar, or any detainee, for that matter, be allowed an opportunity to present a defense, especially when his freedom could be abrogated for the length of the current state of emergency or others that could (and did) follow. The principle of audi alteram partem (let the other side be heard) is a fundamental right in the common law, as is access to legal counsel. To abolish such sacrosanct principles, Parliament would need to explicitly "oust" such rights in the enabling legislation, which it had not done. The state president had no power to revise the regulation to specifically authorize detention without hearing "any person." Such a regulation was "grossly unreasonable, harsh and oppressive," and evidence that the state president had failed to "apply his mind properly" as required by law.[26] The state in response argued that Parliament had indeed provided such discretion to the state president to make such regulations "as appear to him necessary" to preserve public order. There is no constraint on the state president's determination that such a state exists, and once it "appears to him necessary" to declare a state of emergency, any regulations flowing from that assessment are valid, including regulations 3 (3) and 3 (10). Thus Mr. Omar's further detention with no ability to present a defense, according to the state, was lawful.

For the second issue raised, the state argued that the right to access legal counsel was not abolished but merely restricted. Advocate Chaskalson countered that the required consent of the authorities nullified the right of the accused. While Mr. Omar and the other detainees were ultimately granted access to counsel, the reliance on the good will of the state to protect a fundamental liberty is no protection at all.[27]

Advocate Chaskalson's arguments did not convince a majority of the court, but he did succeed in convincing Judge Hoexter. In his dissenting opinion, Judge Hoexter argued that the exclusion of audi alteram partem could apply to the initial detention but not to its further extension. While the power afforded the state president is an "awesome" one it is "not an arbitrary or autocratic" one, he argued.[28] He further agreed with Chaskalson that individuals must have access to legal advisers. Judge Hoexter agreed that under certain circumstances, the state might need to prohibit detainees from access to any individual, including legal advisers. He found less credibility in the state's arguments that those who are detained for their own safety should similarly have no access to legal advisers without permission. Since the state could not, or would not, distinguish between the two types of detainees allowed under the regulations, access to legal advisers must be provided to all of them. Indeed, Judge Hoexter explained in his opinion that he was "unable to assign to Parliament the contemplation of so manifestly indefensible an encroachment on a right which our law properly regards as a fundamental one."[29] Unfortunately for Mr. Omar and the thousands of other detainees, the majority of the panel had no such reservations about Parliament's intention. The court had genuflected to the executive and to Parliament in prior rulings, and the author of the majority's opinion, Chief Justice Rabie, did so here again.[30]

The decision in Mr. Omar's case is the outcome predicted by party capability theory. The national government prevailed and did so in a criminal case. The privileged haves of apartheid South Africa had structured rules and processes to ensure their success. They were the consummate repeat players and enjoyed the power, process, and procedures that allowed them to succeed, especially against those challenging them.

While a democratic South Africa lay ahead, Mr. Omar's fate was determined under an apartheid state and by an apartheid court. Another of the appellants in our data set, Henry Morgentaler, like Mr. Omar, found himself imprisoned by the government, but faced his challenger, the government of Canada, under very different circumstances.

Henry Morgentaler was born in 1953 to a poor Jewish family in Poland. Following the German occupation, he, like many others, was confined to the Jewish ghetto carved out of the city of Lodz, Poland. Unsuccessful in their efforts to hide from the German soldiers driving families of the ghetto to Auschwitz, Henry, his mother, and his brother were transferred to the camp, where his mother ultimately perished.[31] Henry and his brother were later delivered to the Dachau concentration camp, where Henry survived to see the end of the war and his twenty-second birthday in 1945 (Morton 1992, 30–31). Following the war, Henry emigrated to Canada, where he graduated from the University of Montreal in 1953 with a medical degree. After contraception was legalized in

1969, he began specializing in family practice. Given his own background, his sympathy for those ostracized by society should not be surprising. Dr. Morgentaler began a lifelong battle to secure legal access to abortion for women in Canada and did so initially by illegally providing abortions himself (31–33).

In 1969 the Canadian Criminal Code required that women seeking to terminate a pregnancy secure approval from a government-sanctioned hospital's therapeutic abortion committee. If the approval was granted, the abortion had to occur at the hospital that granted it (Martin 2002, 336–37). Believing the legal requirements unjust, Dr. Morgentaler opened a clinic specializing in family practice and began performing abortions (33). Not once, not twice, but three times he was arrested and tried for defiance of the Canadian criminal statute. Not once, not twice, but three times juries acquitted him. In an exceptionally rare move, the initial jury's nullification was overturned in 1974 by the Quebec Court of Appeal,[32] and the court of appeal's action was upheld by the Supreme Court of Canada in 1976.[33] After serving ten months of his eighteen-month sentence, Dr. Morgentaler returned to the practice of medicine undeterred (Morton 1992, 77–87).

After his release from prison, he continued to publicly advocate for the right of any woman to obtain an abortion without interference from the government. He moved to Toronto and, along with two other certified doctors, again opened a clinic to provide abortions, which remained illegal under the Criminal Code. His public violation of the Criminal Code again led to his indictment and a subsequent trial in 1983. Despite their open violation of the Criminal Code, Dr. Morgentaler and his colleagues were acquitted for a fourth time by the jury (Morton 1992, 183–201). The government appealed, and the Court of Appeal of Ontario ordered a new trial. The doctors petitioned for leave to appeal, and more than decade after his original prison sentence was sustained by the Supreme Court, Morgentaler again found himself in front of the justices of the highest court in Canada.

Up to this point, Dr. Morgentaler's experience with the highest court of appeal would have been perfectly predicted by Galanter's party capability theory. The government's success before the Supreme Court was driven by public opinion, public resources, experience, patience, and time. However, Dr. Morgentaler had some advantages of his own by the time of the 1986 appeal. By now, clearly a repeat player, he had gained notoriety, and Canadian public opinion had shifted substantially in support of legalizing abortion (Saurette and Gordon 2015, 120–23). Additionally, the composition of the court had changed substantially. Only two judges from the decision a decade earlier remained on the court, and the first woman, Justice Bertha Wilson, had joined the court in 1982 (Morton 1992, 218). Moreover, the have-not litigants, being medical doctors, were better positioned financially and thus able to hire top-notch counsel to represent them. Morris Manning, the chief counsel for Dr. Morgentaler, held the honorific of Queen's Counsel and had argued many cases before the Supreme Court. Finally, and perhaps most crucially, there had been a critical institutional change since the first *Morgentaler* case. In 1982, Canada adopted the Charter of Rights and Freedoms, which for the first time in Canadian history provided explicit constitutional protection for a wide spectrum of individual rights and liberties. Among the provisions of the charter, section 7 guaranteed the "right to life, liberty and security of the person and the right not to be deprived thereof except in accordance with the principles of fundamental justice." The court ruled 5–2 that the Criminal Code provision severely limiting the right to an abortion was contrary to this new, constitutionally guaranteed right, and thus was null and void.[34] Morgentaler's conviction was therefore overturned, and, unlike Mr. Omar, he walked away a free man.

Mr. Omar and Dr. Morgentaler had their day in vastly different courts. One was in a crumbling authoritarian regime, but a regime where the rules of law were followed and the professionalism of the courts, if not their application of the rules, was respected. The other was in a developed democracy with a history of respect for judicial independence and the rule of law. Yet here too the role of the judiciary was shifting to a more prominent one where its outcomes would set broad policy beyond the freedom of the appellant.

In the previous chapters we explored several ways in which litigants like Mr. Morgentaler or the apartheid regime may or may not have an advantage when presenting their disputes to justices on high courts. While these descriptive analyses offer useful and interesting insights into the dynamics of party capability theory, they all suffer from one significant disadvantage: they examine each country in isolation. It is precisely this disadvantage that permeates the literature. Virtually all the books and articles discussed in chapters 1 and 2 generate conclusions based on single-country research designs. Furthermore, much of the previous research focuses on the US legal system.

While our understanding of courts in the US is instructive, it is critical that we expand our research to other countries and their legal systems. Comparative inquiries allow scholars to control for variation in political, economic, and legal factors that may affect the way in which the capability of parties shapes litigation outcomes. Moreover, it is important to study litigation outcomes over extended periods of time to develop a better understanding of what happens on average and avoid potentially spurious results from analyzing cases from a single point in time. Legal systems emerge and persist in part to peacefully settle conflicts over the rules that govern society, and the context within which these systems develop varies across countries and over time. In this chapter, we seek to understand how that variation affects outcomes in courts; institutions that persist and adapt to changing climates such as by the adoption of a new Charter of Rights and Freedoms in Canada, or by the "authoritarian constitutionalism" of Marcos in the Philippines, or through a post-*Mabo* interpretation of individual rights in Australia, or through the imposition of states of emergency in both India and South Africa.[35] Does it matter that Mr. Omar faced the highest court of appeal in an apartheid South Africa with a developing economy but no rights or liberties for the majority of its citizens? Does it change the party capability calculus that Dr. Morgentaler's appeal was heard by an independent bench in a democratic Canada charged with interpreting the country's newly articulated rights and liberties? If we control for these variations across the countries in our analysis, we generate greater confidence in our findings.

To evaluate the influences that led to Mr. Omar's continued detention and Dr. Morgentaler's release, we pool the data from our sample of individual countries and conduct a series of empirical analyses. Across the six countries (Australia, Canada, the UK, India, the Philippines, and South Africa) there are approximately 14,500 cases, with the decisions per country ranging from 1,522 to 3,065 (mean = 2,423).[36] To account for any unmodeled variation that might exist within specific countries, we employ a series of random effects models (see Gujarati 2003). These models operate similarly to fixed effects models in that they adjust calculations to account for potential heterogeneity in the data caused by the presence of multiple units (i.e., countries) and the unmodeled variation that may exist. The primary advantage of the random effects model is that it allows researchers to include independent variables that do not vary significantly within any single country. Because our various dependent variables (discussed below) are all binary, we rely on random effects logit models to identify systematic influences on court decisions.

Appellant Success Model

In the first empirical specification we examine whether an institutional bias exists that systematically favors appellants over respondents. This allows us to test whether a litigant's net advantage increases the likelihood of success. As we indicated in chapter 3, simply examining the overall success rate may not yield useful insights because of general proclivities to either affirm or reverse the decisions of lower courts. For example, in the US the courts of appeals tend to rule in favor of respondents by affirming the lower court's decisions in approximately 75 percent of cases (Songer and Sheehan 1992), whereas the Supreme Court tends to rule in favor of appellants by reversing approximately 60 percent of appeals (Sheehan, Mishler, and Songer 1992). Wheeler et al. (1987, 407) recognized this potential structural issue when they observed whether a litigant is "better able than other parties to buck the tendency of appellate courts to affirm." As table 14 indicates, in our sample of countries the high courts have a tendency to affirm lower court decisions. Because of this tendency to affirm decisions of the lower courts, our first dependent variable examines the likelihood of an *Appellant Win* (coded 1 = yes, 0 = no).

To directly test the fundamental tenets of party capability theory, we incorporate a series of independent variables related to litigant characteristics. Galanter's (1975) argument focuses on the distinction between repeat players versus one-shotters and haves versus have-nots. The first classification is important because some litigants (especially the national government) have an advantage in experience before the courts. This advantage exists either because of the frequency with which they appear before the judges or because they can afford to lose a single case if that would change the rules in their favor for later decisions. Neither of these advantages exists for one-shot litigants, and therefore Galanter predicts they will lose more often. To measure the difference between these types of litigants, we employ a series of dummy variables, controlling for two litigant categories (coded 1 = yes, 0 = no). Since the national government is the consummate repeat player, we control for those situations in which it appears as the appellant (*National Government as Appellant*) and as the respondent (*National Government as Respondent*). Our expectation is that the presence of the *National Government as Appellant* should significantly increase the likelihood of the appellant winning, while

TABLE 14. High court decision rates by country (%)

	Australia	Canada	UK	India	Philippines	South Africa
Affirm	54.2	57.5	55.3	56.8	63.8	59.9
Reverse	45.8	42.5	44.7	43.2	36.2	40.1

the presence of the *National Government as Respondent* should significantly decrease this likelihood. We also control for the consummate one-shot litigant, the individual, and whether individuals appear as appellants (*Individual as Appellant*) or as respondents (*Individual as Respondent*). Our expectation is that the presence of an *Individual as Appellant* should significantly decrease the likelihood of the appellant winning, whereas the presence of an *Individual as Respondent* should significantly increase this likelihood.

Measuring Galanter's distinction between haves versus have-nots is more difficult since we do not have data on the specific resources committed by litigants to specific cases. Galanter assumes implicitly that the litigant categories themselves serve as sufficient proxies for resources. Thus the national government would always possess more resources than corporations and individuals. While this may be accurate in some instances, some scholars demonstrate where this assumption does not hold (e.g., Chan 2019, Dotan 1999a, 1999b; Haire, Lindquist, and Songer 2003; Haynie 1994, 1995, 2003; He and Su 2013; Sheehan and Randazzo 2012; Smyth 2000; Szmer, Johnson, and Sarver 2007; Tate and Haynie 1994; Yarnold 1995).

As we noted above, both Mr. Omar and Dr. Morgentaler were represented by experienced legal talent, and prior research confirms that experienced attorneys can offset some of the advantages of the haves (e.g., Chen, Huang, and Lin 2014; Haynie and Sill 2007; Sheehan and Randazzo 2012; Szmer, Johnson, and Sarver 2007). We build on these insights by counting the number of attorneys present on the legal team for each litigant. This number ranges from 0 (when litigants represent themselves) to 5 (for large legal teams). To measure the distinction between haves and have-nots, we calculate the variable *Net Attorney Advantage* by subtracting the number of attorneys for the respondent from the number supporting the appellant. The range of this variable runs from −5 (more attorneys for the respondent) to +5 (more attorneys for the appellant). We believe this is a useful proxy measure for haves versus have-nots because of the resources needed to hire attorneys: hiring more attorneys requires more resources to support salaries and related legal expenses. Our expectation is that *Net Attorney Advantage* is positively related to appellants winning.

We also include several control variables, two of which are case-related and five that pertain to country-specific attributes. Among the case-level controls are dummy variables that measure whether the case involves a *Criminal Issue* or a *Civil Liberties Issue* (coded 1 = yes and 0 = no). Our expectation is that both variables will be negatively related to the likelihood of an appellant win. The country-level variables measure specific attributes related either to the judicial system overall or the environment in which courts are situated. The variable *Judicial Independence Index* ranges from 0.000 (no independence) to 1.000 (complete judicial independence) and measures the extent to which the high court possesses independence from other parts of government. This index was developed by Linzer and Staton (2015) to provide an empirical measure that scholars can use to compare levels of judicial independence across countries and over time. The remaining control variables come from the Varieties of Democracy data collected by Coppedge et al. (2017).[37] The variable *Democracy Score* is taken from the United Democracy Score (e_uds_mean) produced by V-Dem, with higher numbers corresponding to greater levels of democracy. The variable *Corruption Score* relates to V-Dem's political corruption index (v2x_corr) and ranges from less corrupt to more corrupt governments. We also include a logged measure of *Per Capita GDP* and a country's *GINI Coefficient* (e_migdppln) to control for the economic conditions and potential income inequality in society. Appendix B provides the descriptive statistics for these variables for each country. Finally, we include temporal fixed effects (in the form of annual dummy variables) to control for any variation over time.[38]

Table 15 presents the results of our initial random effects logit model, which examines the likelihood of an appellant win. The ρ statistic at the bottom of the table indicates that there is a significant amount of unmodeled variation that is appropriately captured by the random effects model. Had we not specified the random effects portion, this unmodeled variation would have biased the empirical results.

Several of the litigant characteristic variables significantly affect the likelihood of an appellant win. The presence of the national government as appellant increases the likelihood of an appellant win, whereas the likelihood significantly decreases when the national government is a respondent. The presence of an individual as appellant has no relation to the likelihood of appellant success; however, when the individual appears as a respondent, the appellant is significantly more likely to win. The results for these dummy variables provide empirical support for Galanter's distinction between repeat players versus one-shotters.

Finally, the variable *Net Attorney Advantage* is significant and positive, indicating that as the number of attorneys representing the appellant increases,

TABLE 15. Likelihood of appellant win (random effects logit)

	Coefficient	Standard error
Litigant characteristics		
National government as appellant	.249***	.065
National government as respondent	−.120**	.047
Individual as appellant	.022	.039
Individual as respondent	.303***	.041
Net attorney advantage	.044**	.018
Case characteristics		
Criminal issue	−.139***	.045
Civil liberties issue	−.197**	.085
Country characteristics		
Judicial independence index	−.508	.356
Democracy score	−.173**	.077
Political corruption score	.453	.422
Per capita GDP	.458***	.096
Gini coefficient	.009*	.004
Constant	−4.249	.787
N	14,540	
Wald χ^2	225.69	
Prob > χ^2	.000	
ρ	.037***	

$^*p < .10, ^{**}p < .05, ^{***}p < .01$. Temporal fixed effects not displayed

the likelihood of an appellant win increases. To illustrate the substantive impact of this variable, we graphed the marginal effects of net attorney advantage in figure 1.

This graph illustrates the influence of attorney advantage on the likelihood of an appellant win. We see that when respondents possess a substantially larger legal team (i.e., when the net attorney advantage is −5), the likelihood of an appellant win is approximately .37. As this net attorney advantage increases in favor of appellants, however, the likelihood of success increases to approximately .47. This supports Galanter's concept that the haves are significantly advantaged over the have-nots during litigation.

While the results from this initial empirical estimation confirm our expectations regarding party capability theory, they do not offer a complete picture. It may be that the effect observed for *Net Attorney Advantage* does not operate

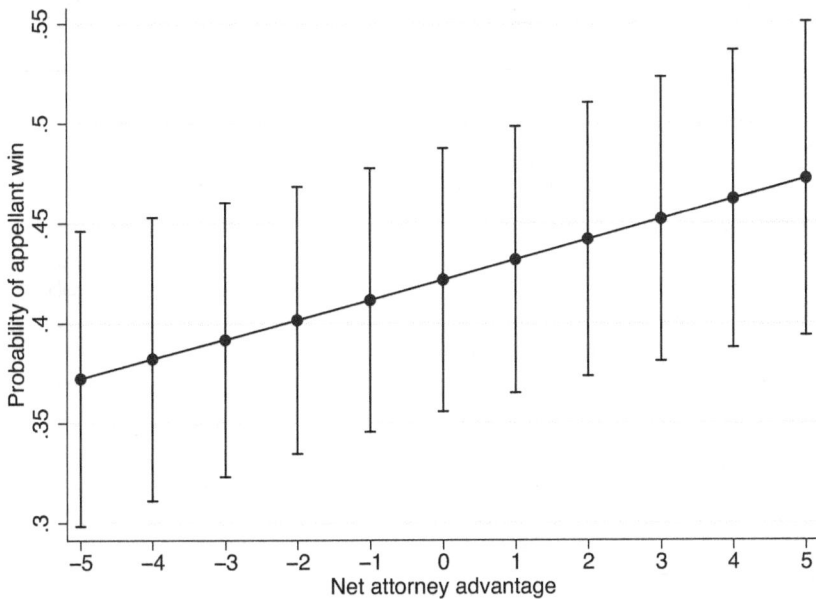

FIGURE 1. Marginal effect of net attorney advantage

equally across all litigants. That is, we suspect that the size of a litigant's legal team may affect the national government differently from businesses and associations as well as for individuals. Therefore, we reran the random effects logit model and included a series of interaction terms to account for this potential differential impact. The results of this specification are reported in table 16.

The results from this specification continue to confirm Galanter's distinction of repeat players versus one-shotters in the same way as the previous specification. However, the more interesting results involve the differential impact of attorney advantage. To see exactly how this variable operates, we graphed the marginal effects separately. Figure 2 captures the substantive impact of the variable *Net Attorney Advantage*. It is important to note that this now measures the influence of attorney advantage for businesses, associations, and state or local government because of the inclusion of the additional interactions.

Figure 2 indicates that these litigants experience a significant advantage by expending resources to hire larger legal teams. Businesses, associations, and state or local government litigants have a .30 probability of success when the

TABLE 16. Likelihood of appellant win with attorney advantage (random effects logit)

	Coefficient	Standard error
Litigant characteristics		
National government as appellant	.252***	.065
National government as respondent	−.120**	.013
Individual as appellant	.018	.039
Individual as respondent	.303***	.041
Net attorney advantage	.107***	.029
Attorney advantage individuals as appellant	−.078**	.039
Attorney advantage national government as appellant	−.161***	.061
Attorney advantage national government as respondent	−.025	.042
Case characteristics		
Criminal issue	−.155***	.046
Civil liberties issue	−.223**	.086
Country characteristics		
Judicial independence index	−.763**	.343
Democracy score	−.334**	.099
Political corruption score	−.662	.579
Per capita GDP	.223*	.125
Gini coefficient	.009	.008
Constant	−1.592	1.455
N	14,540	
Wald χ^2	264.79	
Prob > χ^2	.000	
ρ	.037***	

* $p < .10$, ** $p < .05$, *** $p < .01$. Temporal fixed effects not displayed.

net attorney advantage is at its lowest. However, this probability increases by approximately .15 for each attorney hired (in relation to the respondent's legal team), ultimately reaching a .55 likelihood of success.

Compare this result to that of individuals and their legal teams (represented in figure 3). Here we observe that the marginal effect of additional attorneys adversely influences the likelihood of success when individuals appear as appellants. They move from a .51 probability of success down to a probability of approximately .35. Such a pattern does not conform to Galanter's expectation about resources, though it does support a more basic notion that individuals will always be have-nots, regardless of the resources expended on their legal teams.

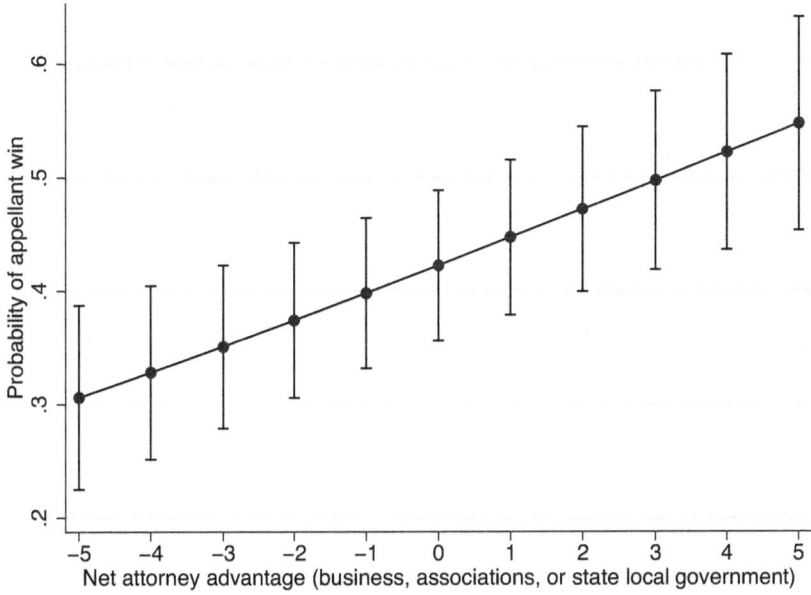

FIGURE 2. Marginal effect of net attorney advantage (businesses, associations, and state/local government)

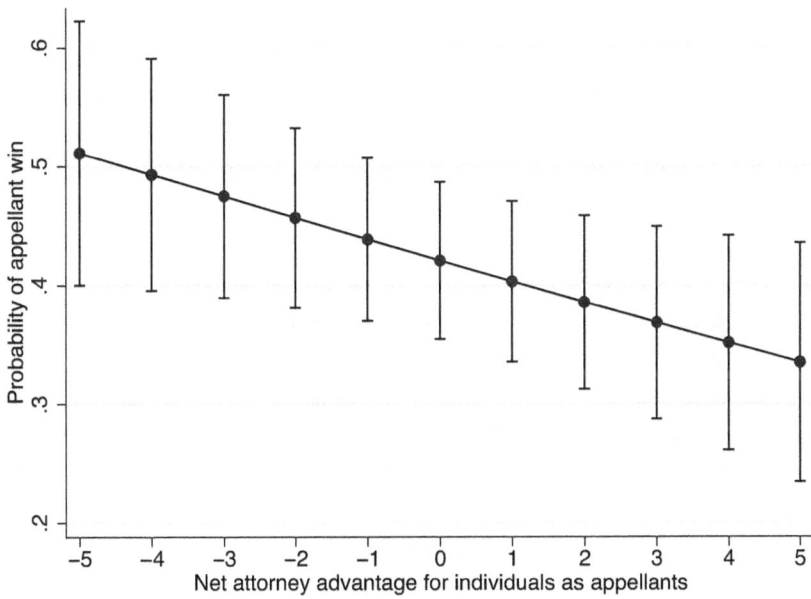

FIGURE 3. Marginal effect of net attorney advantage for individuals as appellants

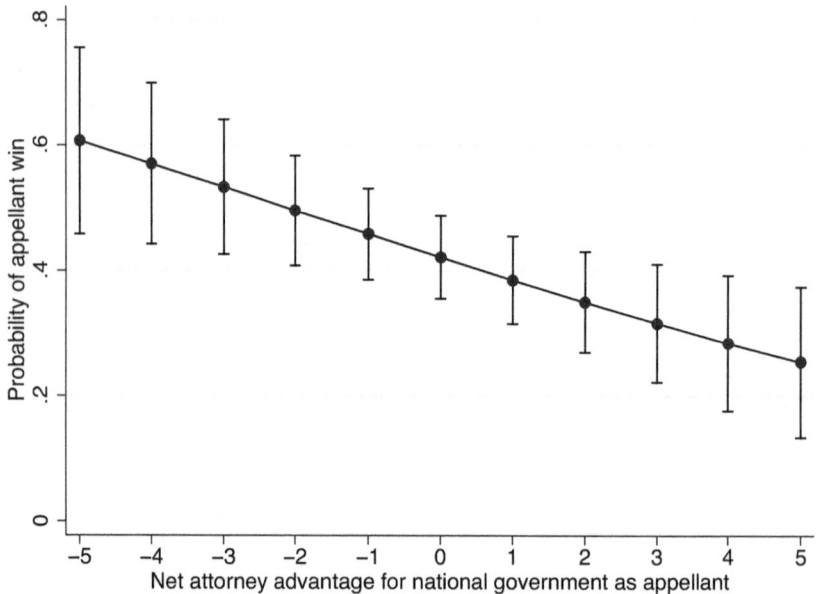

FIGURE 4. Marginal effect of net attorney advantage for national government as appellant

Figure 4 presents the results of attorney advantage for those cases when the national government appears as the appellant. In stark contrast to Galanter's theory about haves versus have-nots and against our own expectations, figure 4 shows a negative relationship between the size of the national government's legal team when the government is the appellant and the likelihood of success. As the net attorney advantage increases in favor of the national government, the probability of winning decreases from .60 to .24. This is a substantial decline for which we can only speculate as to the underlying reason. Perhaps this is attributable to the complexity of the national government's case or to the salience of the issue involved. Since the national government lost in the lower court (hence its status as appellant), it is possible that the larger legal teams occur in high-profile cases where the chances of the government prevailing are small from the start.

When the national government appears as the respondent, we see additional evidence contradicting Galanter's theory concerning haves versus have-nots (figure 5). Increasing the size of the legal team has no meaningful impact on the likelihood of appellant success (the probability decreases from approximately .46 to .39). Therefore, increases in the resources devoted to its legal

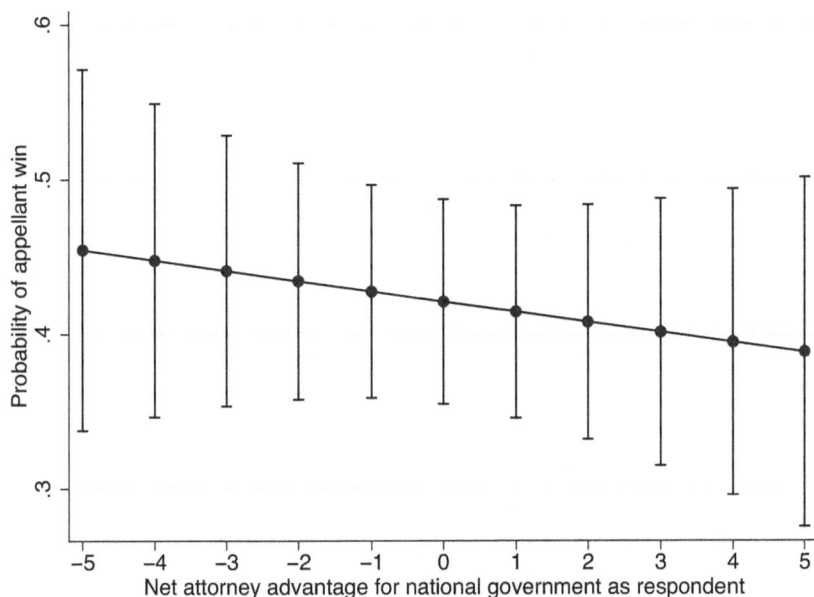

FIGURE 5. Marginal effect of net attorney advantage for national government as respondent

team have no effect on the success of the national government when it appears as the respondent.

In conclusion, the first set of empirical analyses examining the likelihood of appellant success provides mixed support for Galanter's party capability theory. When conceptualizing "capability" in terms of repeat players versus one-shotters, our expectations are confirmed. The national government wins significantly more often regardless of whether it appears as the appellant or as the respondent. Additionally, individuals lose significantly more often when they appear as respondents. However, their appearance as appellants has no meaningful influence on winning.

The picture becomes more complicated when we conceptualize Galanter's theory in terms of haves versus have-nots. Here the evidence is mixed. The only instance where the measure of net attorney advantage adheres to expectations is when we consider businesses, associations, or state and local governments. When these litigants appear as appellants, increases in the size of their legal teams significantly increase the likelihood of success. For individuals, increases in the size of their legal teams adversely affect the likelihood of success. Finally, for the national government, a larger legal team either has a negative impact on its success when appearing as the appellant or has no influence when the government appears as the respondent.

Specific Litigant Success Model

Because of the mixed results derived from examining *Appellant Success* as the dependent variable, we calculate a series of models focused on the success of specific litigants. In model A, *National Government Success,* the dependent variable is the likelihood of the national government winning. Model B, *Individual Success,* uses a dependent variable focused on the likelihood of individuals winning, and model C, *Business/Association Success,* examines the likelihood of these litigants winning. In each model we rely on a random effects probit model to account for both the binary nature of the dependent variable and any variation among countries not explicitly captured by our independent variables. We also include temporal fixed effects (in the form of yearly dummy variables) to control for variation over time.

As in the previous empirical models in this chapter, our primary independent variables capture a range of litigant characteristics to account for any differences between repeat players versus one-shotters and for resource inequalities between the haves and the have-nots. For the former comparison, we include dummy variables measuring whether an *Individual as Appellant* or *Individual as Respondent* appears as the litigant and whether the *National Government as Appellant* or *National Government as Respondent* is present in the case. Galanter's theory leads us to hypothesize that the national government should win both when it appears as an appellant and when it appears as a respondent. Conversely, individuals are more likely to lose regardless of whether they appear as appellants or as respondents.

To control for inequalities between the haves and the have-nots, we include the variable *Litigant Net Attorney Advantage,* which measures the size of the legal team for the litigant in that model (i.e., the *National Government* in model A, *Individuals* in model B, and *Businesses/Associations* in model C) in relation to the opponent's legal team. According to Galanter's prediction, the haves should win significantly more often than the have-nots. Therefore, we hypothesize that *Litigant Net Attorney Advantage* will be positively related to the likelihood of winning. As the size of the legal team relative to the opponent's team increases the likelihood of that specific litigant winning should increase significantly.

We also include several control variables, two of which measure case characteristics. These account for the presence of a *Criminal Issue* or a *Civil Liberties Issue*. We hypothesize the following: in model A, *National Government Success*, the presence of a criminal issue should increase the likelihood of the national government winning, whereas the presence of a civil liberties issue should decrease its chances of success. In model B, *Individual Success*, the presence of a criminal issue should significantly decrease the likelihood of the individual winning. We also include whether or not the case involves a civil liberties issue. Finally, in model C, *Business and Association Success*, the presence of both a criminal issue and a civil liberties issue should decrease the likelihood of businesses and associations winning. Our final set of control variables measure country characteristics. We employ the same country control variables in these models as we used in the previous empirical models: *Judicial Independence Index, Democracy Score, Political Corruption Score, Per Capita GDP,* and the *Gini Coefficient.*

Table 17 displays the results of all three litigant success models. Before examining the effects of specific independent variables, it is important to note that the ρ coefficient in the first two models is statistically significant. This indicates that unmodeled variation related to individual countries exists in the data. Therefore, the random effects probit model is the appropriate choice. For model C, *Business/Association Success*, there is no unmodeled variation related to specific countries. Therefore, we could have simply employed a regular probit model to examine these results. However, for the sake of consistency, we report the random effects probit model in the table.

Table 17 reveals mixed evidence for Galanter's party capability theory. In terms of repeat players versus one-shotters, we would expect the national government to win regardless of whether it appears as the appellant or the respondent (see model A). While this is accurate for the respondent expectation, it does not hold when the national government appears as the appellant.[39] When this situation occurs, the national government is significantly more likely to lose, contrary to the expectation of its repeat player status. Therefore, the strength of the national government seems to exist only in the lower courts: when the national government wins at the lower court, thereby appearing as the respondent before the high court, it is more likely to remain successful. However, if the national government loses in the lower court, its advantage as a repeat player is not sufficient to overcome a disadvantage when it appears as the appellant. Similarly, when individuals appear as appellants against the national government, they are significantly more likely to lose the case. Finally, in terms of haves versus have-nots, a net attorney advantage in

TABLE 17. Likelihood of specific litigant win (random effects probit)

	Model A (National Government Success)	Model B (Individual Success)	Model C (Business/ Associations Success)
Litigant characteristics			
National government as appellant	−.451*** (.121)	−.654*** (.083)	–
National government as respondent	–	−.775*** (.060)	.119 (.089)
Individual as appellant	−.215** (.101)	–	.763*** (.077)
Individual as respondent	.045 (.123)	–	.415*** (.078)
Litigant net attorney advantage	.014 (.032)	.010 (.023)	.050* (.029)
Case characteristics			
Criminal issue	.343*** (.076)	−.189** (.054)	.207 (.169)
Civil liberties issue	.030 (.152)	.092 (.111)	.238 (.175)
Country characteristics			
Judicial independence index	1.145** (.558)	−.162 (.404)	.022 (.409)
Democracy score	.487*** (.148)	−.285** (.097)	−.053 (.102)
Political corruption score	2.509*** (.731)	−1.574*** (.495)	−.191 (.491)
Per capita GDP	.207 (.139)	−.105 (.092)	−.127** (.047)
Gini coefficient	−.002 (.009)	.001 (.006)	−.007 (.005)
Constant	−3.643 (1.746)	−.658 1.312)	.690 (.759)
N	4,525	9,603	5,761
Wald χ^2	139.34	193.68	156.53
Prob > χ^2	.000	.000	.000
ρ	.021***	.007***	.001

*$p < .10$, **$p < .05$, ***$p < .01$. Temporal fixed effects not displayed.

favor of the national government has no statistically significant effect on the likelihood of the national government winning its case. This contradicts our expectation and does not support Galanter's contention.

Model B, *Individual Success*, contains evidence that is more supportive of party capability theory. Here we observe that individuals are significantly more likely to lose when the national government appears either as the appellant or respondent, as we expected. Additionally, the variable *Litigant Net Attorney Advantage* is not statistically significant. This indicates that individuals are not able to rely on hiring larger legal teams as a way to increase their chances of winning.

The final column, model C, *Business/Associations Success,* also offers mixed support for our expectations. When the national government appears as the respondent, there is no significant effect on the likelihood of businesses or associations winning.[40] In contrast, when businesses or associations appear against individuals, they are significantly more likely to win regardless of whether the individual appears as appellant or as respondent. This supports Galanter's hypothesis concerning repeat players versus one-shotters and confirms our expectations. The final variable, *Litigant Net Attorney Advantage* is also statistically significant and positive, demonstrating that businesses and associations can increase their chances of success by securing larger legal teams. To see the substantive impact of this variable, we graphed the marginal effects in figure 6.

Figure 6 indicates that these litigants experience a significant advantage by expending resources to hire larger legal teams. Businesses and associations have just under a .30 probability of success when the net attorney advantage is at its lowest. However, this probability increases by approximately .015 for

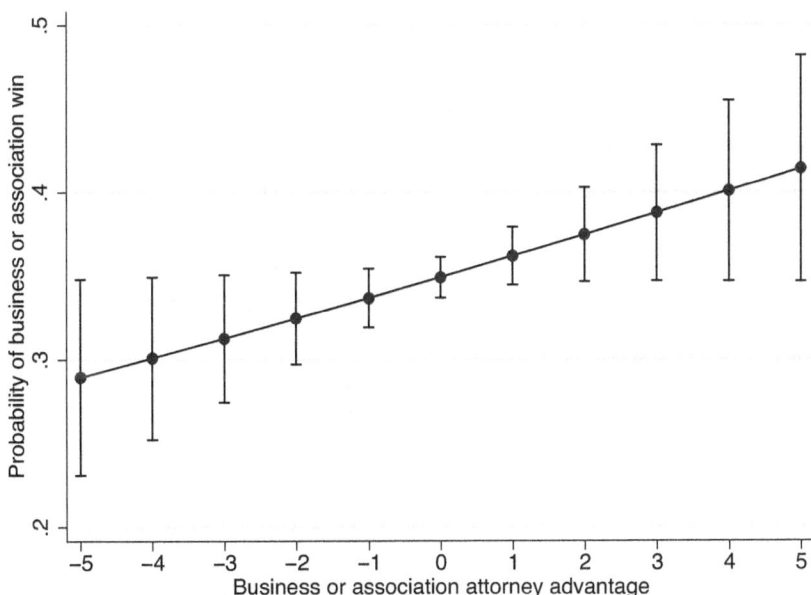

FIGURE 6. Marginal effect of net attorney advantage for businesses and associations

each attorney hired (in relation to the respondent's legal team), ultimately reaching a .42 likelihood of success. This impact supports Galanter's contention that litigants with greater resources (i.e., haves) are more likely to win against opponents with fewer resources (i.e., have-nots).

Discussion

Our models predict that both Mr. Omar and Dr. Morgentaler would face up-hill battles in their appeals. Our models suggest that Mr. Omar would surely lose. He was challenging the national government, the consummate repeat player, in a criminal case with high stakes for the state of emergency. While Mr. Omar assembled an impressive legal team, our *Individual Success* model finds that this would provide no significant return. In the end, as party capability theory would predict, Mr. Omar remained in prison.

For Dr. Morgentaler, our model was less successful in predicting the outcome. Dr. Morgentaler was challenging the national government as an individual and should have been significantly less likely to win, according to party capability theory. However, we expect that the government may face significant challenges in rights and liberties cases like the one Dr. Morgentaler brought before the court. As Haynie (1994, 1995) argues, ruling against the haves may increase the public's support of the court's legitimacy, especially in a case that expands individual liberties.

What we find more critical in our results is that focusing on a single case or two, like that of Mr. Omar or Dr. Morgentaler, limits our ability to advance theory. By expanding our data to include high courts in multiple countries and over extended periods of time, we can have greater confidence that repeat players do experience advantages in courts of law but that those advantages can be tempered, at least for some, by bringing resources, especially greater legal talent, to bear.

It is also important that we consider longer time periods to enhance our confidence. Our model allows us to control for changing political, economic, and legal contexts. Our results persist across nations that become more or less democratic, as economic conditions shift, as levels of corruption rise or fall, or as the independence of courts increases or decreases. Indeed, the Canadian context shifted extensively from Dr. Morgentaler's first arrest in 1970 and his final appearance before the court in 1986 (Morton 1992). The newly adopted Canadian Charter of Rights and Freedoms provided a new avenue to expand rights and liberties for Canadian citizens. Dr. Morgentaler's decades-long fight to secure a woman's right to a legal abortion was finally supported by the highest court of appeal. The majority opinion found the criminal statute to be a "profound interference with a woman's body and thus an infringement of the security of the person" guaranteed in the charter.[41] Justices McIntyre and La Forest disagreed, arguing that there is no right to abortion in either the Charter of Rights and Freedoms or in Canadian "law, custom or tradition."[42] Fortunately for Dr. Morgentaler, that sentiment did not prevail.

For Mr. Omar, as a one-shotter seeking his freedom against the repeat player of the apartheid government, a loss was expected, but, as we argue, it is important to control for changing contexts and for time. Shortly after the court's decision, apartheid would collapse. Nelson Mandela would be released from prison a little over three decades after Mr. Omar had defended him in the Rivonia trial. Democratic elections would follow, along with a new constitution and a new democratic regime with Mandela at its helm. Mr. Omar would be appointed its inaugural minister of justice. The advocate who defended him, Arthur Chaskalson, would be appointed chief justice of the newly created Constitutional Court.

The political contexts for both Mr. Omar and Dr. Morgentaler changed over the course of their lives. Those who were the repeat players, the one-shotters, the haves, and the have-nots shifted over time, but at least for some, the advantages identified by party capability persisted regardless of the rules or the rulers. Our comparative analysis gives us greater confidence in our ability to understand winners and losers in courts of law.

6 | Repeat Players, One-Shotters, and More

There are many pleasant fictions of the law in constant operation, but there is not one so pleasant or practically humorous as that which supposes every man to be of equal value in its impartial eye, and the benefits of all laws to be equally attainable by all men, without the smallest reference to the furniture of their pockets.

—Charles Dickens, *Nicholas Nickleby*

WE STARTED THE book with this quotation from Charles Dickens. In the early 1800s he recognized that equality under the law was an ideal, and that those individuals with greater resources possessed a distinct advantage. With the evolution of modern political science, generations of scholars and practitioners have more thoroughly investigated this dynamic to better understand who wins and who loses. Indeed, Galanter's own speculation on the limits of legal change arose from his experiences with the Indian legal system, where he observed the inequality between the haves and the have-nots and the consequences of those differences for litigation outcomes.

Like many scholars of his era, Galanter sought reforms that would maximize the redistributive power of courts. Providing legal aid to those who could not afford it was seen as crucial to offsetting the inherent imbalance between the haves and the have-nots Galanter identified. Our results suggest that the efforts of Galanter and other scholars and practitioners of the time to address the imbalance of social power through litigation was less than successful. What Galanter did accomplish with his seminal article was to create one of the most cited law review articles in history. Shapiro's (2021) study finds Galanter second among the most cited law and social science scholars. In his evaluation of the article's impact, Talesh (2014) suggests it was "seminal, blockbuster, canonical, game-changing, extraordinary, pivotal, and noteworthy" (iii).

It is not common for a single piece of scholarly writing to have such an influence on a single discipline, but this essay's impact crosses multiple disciplines and has shaped research that encompasses political science, law, sociology, criminology, and anthropology. As our literature review in chapters 2 and 3 demonstrates, party capability theory arguably is one of the most tested legal theories.

This book makes a significant contribution through our comprehensive evaluation of almost fifty years of studies focusing on party capability theory. The proliferation of studies analyzing who wins and who loses is exceptional not only for the sheer number of studies but also for the broad range of analyses that have been conducted. The repeat player hypothesis has been tested in civil and criminal courts, trial and appellate courts, specific areas of law, and national and international courts, and the repeat player variable extends to many other analyses of judicial decision-making. Our literature review is extensive, and while we make no claims we have covered every study involving the repeat player hypothesis, we do believe our evaluation of the literature enables us to identify and test the common themes.

The comparative analysis of this book also helps to advance the generalizability of party capability theory. Galanter's theory correctly predicts Mr. Moorthy's experience before the Supreme Court of India. The government, as Galanter theorizes, was interested in the long game and in shaping public policy. Party capability theory also correctly predicts that Andrew Johnson would not succeed against his insurance company, that the developers would prevail in their venture at the Canary Wharf, and that the apartheid government would prevail in its detention of Mr. Omar. However, according to party capability theory, Augustina's family should not have prevailed in their challenge, nor should Mr. Morgentaler have been able to overcome multiple guilty verdicts. Understanding single case outcomes can help to develop our theories, but to have confidence in their ability to explain and predict outcomes requires applying our theories across multiple systems at various stages of political, economic, and legal development for many years. Our results find mixed support for Galanter's theory.

We find substantial support for Galanter's underlying hypothesis that those parties who have greater capability prevail. Parties such as the government can both shape the law and the individuals who staff the law's implementation and application. Businesses and associations similarly succeed because of the greater resources typically available to them. They too can shape the law by settling cases that may create negative precedents and pressing those that will not, and they can do so by hiring substantial legal talent to advocate for them. Individuals, who most often bring only single legal challenges, lack the financial means, the experience, or the time to play the long game. As a result, their ability to challenge those who do is daunting. As Galanter (1975) notes, "Law in America is a complex and expensive activity requiring employment of full-time specialists . . . and almost all individuals are too poor to play" (346).

With the exception of the Philippines, we find that on average, the government does win more often than not, but the government's opponents can and do prevail across countries. These aggregate results are influenced by individual issues areas. Indeed, it appears that while courts are deferential overall to the haves, and especially to the national government, there are issue areas where courts are supportive of the have-nots. Individuals bringing tort claims have greater success in Australia, Canada, South Africa, and especially India. Even under apartheid South Africa, those individuals who brought rights and liberties claims against the regime had a positive net advantage. Individuals bringing private economic claims enjoy some measure of success overall in Canada and India. The government struggles to prevail consistently in criminal cases in Australia and South Africa but succeeds much more often in the UK and especially in Canada.

Overall, the analyses in chapters 3 and 4 provide nuanced support for party capability theory across national high courts. The one consistent finding is that in general, governments are more successful in litigation, as we would expect, but individuals generally do better than predicted in these courts, a finding that the repeat player hypothesis cannot explain. Surprisingly, corporations have mixed success rates across the countries and often are at a net disadvantage when opposing individuals. Litigation in the highest appellate courts may be more complicated than the routine experienced in the lower courts. High courts appreciate their institutional role. As Haynie (1994, 1995, 2004) suggests, they may find legal niches where their decisions favor the have-nots. We find this observation holds across the countries we studied. Future research should examine more closely whether or not courts utilize legal niches to increase their legitimacy as political institutions. Consistently ruling against the have-nots to favor the haves could affect the perception of the legitimacy of courts and indeed of the rule of law. As Haynie notes, courts are unlikely to challenge the regime in the handful of high-profile cases in any given year, but the remainder of the docket provides ample space to favor the have-nots in issue areas that do not threaten the balance of power among political institutions. We are not suggesting that decisions are driven without consideration of the facts and the law, but we do argue that judges are political actors and are cognizant of their pivotal role. Courts that persistently favor the haves could undermine the public's perception of their authority to resolve conflicts, and that concern can shift as context shifts. Challenging the apartheid government in Mr. Omar's detention would have posed a greater threat to the court and to the regime than overturning Dr. Morgentaler's conviction in Canada during a post-charter landscape. The value of the cross-national approach is the ability to develop a multivariate comparative model across the shifting contexts of our countries.

Although we cannot account for all variables that might affect litigant outcomes in the courts, the advantage of a cross-national design over previous single-country studies is that we can develop a statistical model that controls for political, economic, and legal factors that may influence the role of party capability in litigant success. The multivariate models allow us to determine the impact of repeat player status and of resources on success. Galanter's theory predicts that those who have greater resources will prevail. One of the most critical resources he identifies is repeated appearances in court. Those who are in court more often, the repeat players, have greater understanding of the rules, of how to navigate the legal system, and of its staff. Repeat players, typically businesses, associations, and, of course, the government, can elect to settle cases they are likely to lose and persist with those that can create favorable precedents for future cases. The haves typically are those who have the resources to become repeat players or to access those who already are. By contrast, one-shotters represent most individuals or small businesses, who may face a litigant in court on only a single occasion. They do not know the legal system or its terrain well and care only about their case. They are not concerned about future precedents or changing the complex legal landscape.

Our statistical models provide results consistent with party capability theory. Using businesses and associations as a baseline for comparison, when the national government is the challenger or is being challenged, it enjoys greater success. Also as predicted by the repeat player hypothesis, we find that when individuals, the proto-typical one-shotters, are appellants, there is no significant impact on appellant success, and when individuals are respondents, there is a greater probability of the appellant winning. Individuals, as Galanter predicts, are less likely to succeed in general.

How can litigants combat the advantages of repeat players? Galanter suggests that procuring legal talent may help one-shotters offset the advantages of repeat players. However, it may also be that the haves can exacerbate their repeat player status by accessing more and better legal advocates. Our findings clarify the distinction between repeat players and one-shotters and the haves and the have-nots. The national government as the ultimate repeat player and having access to substantial resources should enjoy an overwhelming advantage, but we find this is not true when the government appears as the appellant before the high court. It seems that losing in the lower courts creates a disadvantage for national governments that more experience and greater resources cannot consistently overcome. Individuals lose when the national government is the respondent, but when the national government is appealing a lower court loss to an individual there is no disadvantage for the individual winning or losing before the high court. The net attorney advantage variable also is not significant: more legal talent does not affect the success of individuals in the high courts. In fact, the results suggest that the government's repeat player status provides greater advantages for the government than does securing more lawyers. The latter actually decreases the likelihood of success. However, businesses benefit significantly from their ability to hire more attorneys and presumably higher-quality attorneys. Repeat players such as the government do enjoy the advantage Galanter predicts across a variety of legal systems. However, repeat players such as businesses and associations that hire larger legal teams are indeed the haves who prevail in litigation outcomes.

Advancing Party Capability Theory

Our objectives in writing this book were twofold. One was to consolidate the extensive body of research conducted over decades on party capability theory and to identify commonalities and inconsistencies in the studies. This tracking of the evolution of the theory across time allows us to refine its application in our analyses. We believe it is the most comprehensive review of the literature to date. We also sought to extend party capability theory to the decisions of high courts by providing the first comparative analysis of Galanter's classic argument.

Our study advances party capability theory in several important ways. It demonstrates that the theory can help us understand litigant outcomes in a comparative perspective. There is no reason to suspect our countries are unique. In fact, we provide analyses of countries with varying political, economic, and legal environments. We hope to see future research exploring and expanding the focus to comparative analyses of other legal systems and at other levels. Our focus on appellate courts is critical, but the vast majority of litigation occurs in trial courts. We encourage scholars to pursue truly comparative studies at the trial court level.

In addition, while party capability theory may be viewed as intuitive—

those with more, prevail—our findings indicate that explaining litigation outcomes is not that simplistic. A case in point is the differences we find between the repeat player versus one-shotter and the have versus have-not hypotheses. Scholars often conflate the two or use the terms interchangeably. However, it is important to distinguish between these different dimensions. They are both part of the explanation for why some litigants are more likely to win than others, but future studies need to control for the effects of repeated experiences in litigation compared to potentially different effects based on resources.

We also confirm that national governments enjoy the success Galanter predicts, but their advantage is not unequivocal. Governments enjoy greater success in some areas than others. Future research should explore those legal niches where the have-nots and the one-shotters enjoy greater success. Our results indicate that businesses that can secure a net attorney advantage can succeed at significantly higher rates. However, the national government's status as a repeat player is not affected by bringing greater resources to bear through increasing the size of its legal team. An individual's one-shotter status cannot be overcome regardless of the size of their legal team. This is contrary to Galanter's prediction. Those who can procure greater legal talent should see greater success, but our findings demonstrate that this advantage varies by litigant and by repeat player status.

In summary, we see our analyses providing support for party capability theory across our six countries, with some important caveats. The national government wins more often through its litigation experience and the institutional relationship between the government, the law, and the high courts. This supports party capability theory and the repeat player hypothesis. At the same time, we find evidence for the importance of litigant resources in our haves versus have-nots analysis, with businesses having greater success rates when they have a net advantage in attorneys. Finally, we find that individuals before the high courts have mixed results but in general are not as successful, especially when issue area is controlled for. Individuals face significant challenges in criminal cases. They fare much better in civil cases in our analyses, a finding that is also true of the US Supreme Court (Sheehan, Mishler, and Songer 1992).

Conclusion

Legal systems emerge and persist to resolve the claims of individual litigants. Andrew Johnson secures insurance to protect himself against risk and yet fails to convince the court that he lost the use of his foot as a foot. Resources are expended to create precedents that either extend or limit liability. The insurance company with its repeated defense against the claims of individuals like Andrew, and the company's ability to support large legal teams in its efforts, aligns perfectly with Galanter's hypotheses and our own findings. Businesses that develop properties advancing their economic interests can leverage prior precedents and navigate or avoid local ordinances and permitting processes with large legal teams, as did the developers of the Canary Wharf. Galanter predicts their success, and our models confirm it. But what of Dr. Morgentaler? Despite the government bringing all its resources to bear against him, and doing so repeatedly, it failed. Dr. Morgentaler enjoyed shifting legal terrain that allowed him to overcome the advantages of the repeat player, and indeed, over time he became one himself. How do we explain Augustina's family succeeding despite no studies linking her work to her cancer? The ultimate one-shotters, Augustina's family prevailed when party capability theory would not have predicted it would do so. As we note, courts understand that the law must be seen as an avenue for those who have less to prevail. Further, Galanter and many scholars of his generation saw the legal system as a pathway for social change, a pathway for addressing social inequality. As Rosenberg (1991) finds, the American legal system represented a hollow hope for those who sought social change through its courts.

Our findings suggest that not all hope is lost, but that the challenge to overcome the structural advantages Galanter identifies persists. That hope is embodied in the case of Mr. Omar. In his attempts to challenge an unjust system, he found an unsympathetic court in his efforts to bring about social change. Ultimately, Mr. Omar prevailed in ways Galanter could not have predicted. The apartheid regime of South Africa was followed by a democratic one, in which Mr. Omar would play a pivotal role. In 1990 he became the director of the Community Law Centre at the University of the Western Cape and an important intellectual architect of the new constitutional order. In 1994 he was elected to parliament in the first democratic election in South Africa. He was then appointed by Nelson Mandela to be minister of justice and was responsible for transforming the apartheid era judiciary into a new legal order that could sustain the rule of law in the new rights-based constitutional framework. He would now be responsible for administering justice for the repeat players and the one-shotters, the haves and the have-nots.

Appendix A

DESCRIPTIONS OF THE HIGH COURTS

The National High Courts Database was created with funding from the National Science Foundation.[1] These countries were selected primarily because of their shared common law heritage and because they represent a variety of geographic regions. From the North Atlantic the data set includes Canada and the United Kingdom. From the Asia-Pacific region, Australia, India, and the Philippines were selected, three nations that manifest sharp differences in economic standing and in ethnic, linguistic, and religious composition. Finally, South Africa provides a multi-ethnic nation with a distinctive history of nondemocratic rule. For efficiency, these countries were selected either because the opinions were published in English or because English translations were available. We believe these courts provide a desirable sample for comparative inquiry.

The inclusion of the Philippines, South Africa, the United Kingdom, and Australia was also partially dictated by research efficiency since the principal investigators had done substantial field research in these countries and had acquired substantial expertise. Aside from these considerations—the Anglo-American tradition, English usage, geographic regions, and country expertise—these countries exhibit remarkable differences among a wide variety of social, economic, and political characteristics. Below we provide very brief sketches of the high courts included in the data set. These descriptions are intentionally brief in light of our goal of comparative inquiry rather than single-country studies. Moreover, our empirical models include variables that account for both economic variation and variation in judicial structure and function, democratization, and political corruption. Thus we do not include below discussions of these variables for each country across the decades of our study but focus on basic structure and jurisdiction. Volumes have been written on the high courts of each of these countries. Comprehensive discussions are beyond the scope of this book.

The Supreme Court of Canada was established by the Supreme Court Act passed by Parliament in 1875. Nine justices sit on the court in Ottawa, Ontario, led by the chief justice of Canada. The justices are appointed by the governor in council "for terms of good behavior," so generally for life. The governor in council refers to the governor general, who acts on advice given by the federal cabinet. The court is a general court of appeal from all other Canadian courts and has jurisdiction in constitutional law and all other areas of law. The court has discretionary jurisdiction, and the majority of the cases are heard under a grant of leave. There are some special jurisdiction situations where right of appeal is mandated but it is a limited part of the docket. A major change for the Canadian court system in 1982 was the adoption of a Charter of Rights.

The High Court of Australia was established in the constitution adopted in 1901. The appointment of justices and the first sitting of the court had to wait until the passage of the Judiciary Act in 1903. The High Court is in Canberra and the court sits in three courtrooms, depending on the matter before the court and the number of justices hearing the case. The court consists of seven justices led by the chief justice. When a vacancy occurs, the attorney-general presents a name to the cabinet, which then recommends the appointment of a new justice to the governor-general. The process is generally considered apolitical and receives little attention from the public. Justices are required to retire at the age of seventy. The High Court of Australia has discretionary jurisdiction, and most cases are heard after the granting of special leave to appeal by the court. There is no automatic right to appeal to the High Court but there are a small number of cases that can originate in the court. A significant change for the discretionary jurisdiction of the court occurred in 1984 with the abolishment of appeals to the Privy Council.

The Appellate Committee of the House of Lords was in existence during the period of our analysis for the UK. The committee consisted of twelve lords of appeal in ordinary, who were judges having membership in the House of Lords of Parliament. The lords of appeal in ordinary were required to retire at age seventy or seventy-five, depending on when they were first appointed to office. During our time period of analysis the majority were under the age of seventy-five rule. The jurisdiction of the Appellate Committee was governed by the Appellate Jurisdiction Act of 1876, which limited appeals to only important cases, but interestingly, the law lords did not have the power of judicial review of parliamentary acts. Cases were usually heard by five lords of appeal, but the number could vary since there was no one appellate committee for a case. A committee would be formed when there was a case to be heard. The ruling of an appellate committee was final, even though the House of Lords technically could reconsider a decision. That rarely happened. The Supreme Court of the UK was created in 2009 and replaced this appellate committee.

The Supreme Court of India is the final arbiter in legal disputes, with original jurisdiction over cases between the central government and the states and cases between states. The court enjoys appellate jurisdiction over both criminal and civil cases arising from the eighteen high courts as well as from the lower subdistrict and village courts. The president can refer cases for advisory opinions. Cases arise as well from the fundamental freedoms articulated in the constitution. Members of the Supreme Court consist of a chief justice and a maximum of thirty-four judges. The court typically sits in panels of three, but panel size can vary, depending on the case. Judges are appointed by the president of India after consultation with members of the Supreme Court and judges of the state high courts as the president deems necessary. Once appointed, judges enjoy protection of tenure and remuneration. Judges must retire at the age of sixty-five.

The Philippine Supreme Court sits atop the hierarchical legal structure of the Philippines, which consists of municipal, regional, and appellate courts, including specialized courts with jurisdiction over taxation and corruption and sharia courts, which exercise limited jurisdiction over Muslim populations in certain sections of the country. The Supreme Court enjoys discretionary jurisdiction over all lower courts with a few exceptions for mandatory appeals, for example of death sentences. The Supreme Court is comprised of a chief justice and fourteen associate justices. The court can sit en banc but does so rarely. The size of the panels, typically three, five, or seven, is at the discretion of the court. Justices are appointed by the president and serve until the age of seventy and enjoy protection of tenure and of their salaries.

South Africa's highest court of appeal for the majority of our time frame was the Appellate division, now Supreme Court of Appeal (see below). The Appellate Division/Supreme Court of Appeal consists of a chief justice and a number of judges of appeal, expanding to eighteen by 1990, though statutory provisions allow for the appointment by the chief justice of acting judges for short periods of time. The court sits in panels of three for criminal cases, though panels of five are assigned for particularly complex criminal cases. The civil cases are heard by panels of five judges. While the court can sit en banc, it does so very rarely. The court enjoys broad discretion over cases appealed from the provincial courts. Judges are selected by the prime minister after consultation with the minister of justice and informally with the chief justice. Judges enjoy security of tenure until mandatory retirement age of seventy. It should be noted that the Appellate Division was replaced by the Supreme Court of Appeal under the new democratic dispensation. The 1994 Constitution designated the Supreme Court of Appeal as the highest court of appeal in nonconstitutional matters, and initially the Supreme Court of Appeal considered itself an equivalent to the Constitutional Court rather than subject to its purview. That fiction was allayed when the Constitutional Court overturned a decision of the Supreme Court of Appeal in *Bannatyne v. Bannatyne and Another* (2002) 2003 (2) SALR 363. The Constitutional Court reversed a decision of the Supreme Court of Appeal involving nonpayment of maintenance support for two children. Our analyses include only the decisions of the Appellate Division/Supreme Court of Appeal, the highest court of appeal persisting over the three decades of the analysis.

Appendix B

DESCRIPTIVE STATISTICS FOR THE INDIVIDUAL HIGH COURTS

TABLE A1. Descriptive statistics for random effects logit model

	Mean	Standard deviation	Minimum	Maximum
Litigant characteristics				
National government as appellant	0.085	0.279	0	1
National government as respondent	0.268	0.443	0	1
Individual as appellant	0.537	0.498	0	1
Individual as respondent	0.303	0.459	0	1
Net attorney advantage	−0.036	0.968	−5	5
Country characteristics				
Judicial independence index	0.762	0.234	0.159	0.986
Democracy score	0.742	0.797	−0.982	2.094
Political corruption score	0.324	0.280	0.031	0.875
Per capita GDP	8.507	1.111	6.725	10.061
Gini coefficient	37.111	9.185	22.350	63.000

TABLE A2. Descriptive statistics for random effects logit model—Australia

	Mean	Standard deviation	Minimum	Maximum
Litigant characteristics				
National government as appellant	0.075	0.264	0	1
National government as respondent	0.283	0.451	0	1
Individual as appellant	0.459	0.498	0	1
Individual as respondent	0.235	0.424	0	1
Net attorney advantage	−0.107	0.861	−4	4
Country characteristics				
Judicial independence index	0.980	0.004	0.972	0.986
Democracy score	10741	0.221	10389	2.094
Political corruption score	0.047	0.000	0.047	0.047
Per capita GDP	9.658	0.174	9.394	10.028
Gini coefficient	29.261	4.035	22.350	37.600

$N = 1,893$.

TABLE A3. Descriptive statistics for random effects logit model—Canada

	Mean	Standard deviation	Minimum	Maximum
Litigant characteristics				
National government as appellant	0.061	0.240	0	1
National government as respondent	0.141	0.349	0	1
Individual as appellant	0.517	0.499	0	1
Individual as respondent	0.261	0.439	0	1
Net attorney advantage	0.003	0.914	−4	4
Country characteristics				
Judicial independence index	0.942	0.030	0.867	0.969
Democracy score	1.391	0.095	1.041	1.558
Political corruption score	0.052	0.006	0.046	0.061
Per capita GDP	9.753	0.171	9.385	10.060
Gini coefficient	31.601	2.361	28.050	37.950

$N = 3,086$.

TABLE A4. Descriptive statistics for random effects logit model — England

	Mean	Standard deviation	Minimum	Maximum
Litigant characteristics				
National government as appellant	0.132	0.339	0	1
National government as respondent	0.235	0.424	0	1
Individual as appellant	0.394	0.488	0	1
Individual as respondent	0.268	0.443	0	1
Net attorney advantage	0.048	0.821	−5	5
Country characteristics				
Judicial independence index	0.895	0.067	0.755	0.965
Democracy score	1.370	0.161	1.121	1.662
Political corruption score	0.044	0.002	0.031	0.048
Per capita GDP	9.617	0.205	9.264	9.999
Gini coefficient	30.528	3.424	23.400	35.500

$N = 1,565$.

TABLE A5. Descriptive statistics for random effects logit model — India

	Mean	Standard deviation	Minimum	Maximum
Litigant characteristics				
National government as appellant	0.076	0.265	0	1
National government as respondent	0.260	0.438	0	1
Individual as appellant	0.587	0.492	0	1
Individual as respondent	0.343	0.474	0	1
Net attorney advantage	0.018	1.278	−5	5
Country characteristics				
Judicial independence index	0.664	0.026	0.632	0.740
Democracy score	0.653	0.155	0.202	0.822
Political corruption score	0.378	0.065	0.314	0.526
Per capita GDP	7.050	0.256	6.725	7.540
Gini coefficient	31.848	2.430	28.400	41.600

$N = 3,215$.

TABLE A6. Descriptive statistics for random effects logit model—Philippines

	Mean	Standard deviation	Minimum	Maximum
Litigant characteristics				
National government as appellant	0.084	0.278	0	1
National government as respondent	0.391	0.488	0	1
Individual as appellant	0.694	0.460	0	1
Individual as respondent	0.393	0.488	0	1
Net attorney advantage	−0.081	0.886	−5	4
Country characteristics				
Judicial independence index	0.375	0.149	0.159	0.571
Democracy score	−0.041	0.660	−0.982	0.686
Political corruption score	0.773	0.090	0.658	0.875
Per capita GDP	7.668	0.082	7.475	7.791
Gini coefficient	44.579	3.336	39.433	50.500

$N = 3,065$.

TABLE A7. Descriptive statistics for random effects logit model—South Africa

	Mean	Standard deviation	Minimum	Maximum
Litigant Characteristics				
National government as appellant	0.105	0.306	0	1
National government as respondent	0.294	0.456	0	1
Individual as appellant	0.451	0.497	0	1
Individual as respondent	0.268	0.443	0	1
Net attorney advantage	−0.106	0.796	−3	4
Country Characteristics				
Judicial independence index	0.897	0.028	0.856	0.938
Democracy score	−0.173	0.395	−0.543	0.604
Political corruption score	0.430	0.037	0.353	0.457
Per capita GDP	8.294	0.064	8.169	8.407
GINI Coefficient	52.297	5.629	45.000	63.000

$N = 2,384$.

Introduction

1. Because we are interested in litigation outcomes, we do not assess individual judges' votes.
2. Compiling the National High Courts Database was funded by the National Science Foundation under the following grants: "Fitting More Pieces into the Puzzle of Judicial Behavior: A Multi-Country Data Base and Program of Research," SES No. 9975237, awarded in 2000 to Co-Investigators Stacia L. Haynie, Louisiana State University; C. Neal Tate, University of North Texas; Reginald Sheehan, Michigan State University; and Donald Songer, University of South Carolina; "Extending a Multi-Country Data Base and Program of Research," SES No. 0137055, awarded for 2002–2006 to Co-Investigators Stacia L. Haynie, Louisiana State University; C. Neal Tate, University of North Texas; Reginald Sheehan, Michigan State University; and Donald Songer, University of South Carolina. Because we are not interested in single-country studies, we do not provide extensive descriptions of the six high courts included in our study. However, we do provide brief descriptions of each in appendix A, along with the selection criteria for these countries.

1. Party Capability Theory in the United States

1. We discuss below the role of government in litigation outcomes, but we should note that the authors find that this effect diminishes when the government is present. The government is more likely to achieve a decisive victory.
2. Though we do not evaluate their analysis here, Priest and Klein (1984) suggest that the certainty provided in settlements will lead to a 50 percent probability of success for any individual plaintiff in the uncertain world of litigation, but they and other scholars (see, e.g., Hylton 1993) find varying support for their econometric model.
3. See Edelman and Suchman (1999, 2003) for an insightful discussion of organizations' annexation of lawlike processes such as mandating the use of alternative dispute resolution, the use of in-house counsel, and the use of private policing, including drug testing, employee surveillance, and protection. The authors argue that the "legalization of organizational governance" has transformed "the large bureaucratic organization from being merely a repeat player in the public legal system to being an entire private legal system in its own right. . . . The power of repeat players to win disputes and to structure transactions, which Galanter discussed in 1974, simply pales by comparison to the new power that arises when the 'haves' hold court" (Edelman and Suchman 1999, 985).
4. Bingham (1998) subsequently analyzed judicial review as a potential avenue of eliminating repeat player bias in arbitration awards. The Supreme Court has ruled in *Commonwealth Coatings Corporation v. Continental Casualty Company* (393 U.S. 145 (1968)) that a reviewing court should vacate an award for "evident partiality." Bingham recognizes the problem confronting the structural bias Galanter articulated

because of the difficulty in statistically demonstrating bias, much less substantively doing so. Judicial review is thus a potential counterbalance to the haves-prone system but has significant limitations.

5. Burch (2017) and Burch and Williams (2017) argue to the contrary that the dominance of a narrow group of repeat player plaintiff and respondent attorneys in these large MDL cases can lead to perverse outcomes where attorneys play for the rules that financially benefit them rather than work on behalf of their clients.

6. Gray and Lowery (1995) find that more interest group representation results in the enactment of more laws, though they are unable to test the ability of groups to achieve their desired content.

7. Other works noting significant effects of campaign contributions on legislative behavior include Feldstein and Melnick (1984), Coughlin (1985), Ashford (1986), Jones and Keiser (1987), and Quinn and Shapiro (1991). Others find few or mixed effects (Kau and Rubin 1981; Langbein 1986; Neustadtl 1990; Owens 1986; Rothenberg 1992; Welch 1982).

8. See, e.g., Roots's (2010) discussion of the development of the federal rules of procedure, which greatly favor the US government. Roots cites the fact that the federal government is given a variety of filing advantages over private sector parties. Roots sees these advantages as violations of the ideals of due process and equal protection. Both Shapiro and Galanter would see the development of the rules in a manner that favors the government as predictable, and the fact that the government wins more often as a result of the rules predictable as well. In terms of businesses shaping the rules to their advantage, Shaffer (2009) argues that businesses have gained recognition before courts as "persons" and have been able to exploit that recognition to their advantage.

9. We recognize that many state courts judges are elected. Presumably, deference is to the electorate rather than to the "government" per se, but since the electorate staffs the government as well, the preferences of the regime should be conflated with those of the judges.

10. Myers and Downey (2017) also find that subnational governments have greater success against local governments. However, their analysis of the Canadian and Australian highest courts of appeal finds variation in the outcomes in those high courts. The national government in Canada has much greater success against local governments and the Australian national government much less.

2. Party Capability Theory in a Comparative Context

1. We would also argue that Toharia's (1975) study of judicial independence in Spain provides support for Galanter's thesis, though Toharia does not specifically engage Galanter's work in his own theoretical framework. He nonetheless finds that judges may be independent, but their independence provides no power to combat the advantages of the government. Substantive legal challenges were not the province of the courts. The authoritarian regime of Franco afforded the courts independence because "they are powerless" (486). Toharia's work confirms the assertions of Shapiro that courts are extensions of the government but goes further to argue that

courts in authoritarian regimes are even more constrained. Toharia is one of many scholars who have evaluated judicial decision-making in a comparative context. This section is by no means exhaustive of the comparative judicial politics research but is meant to focus on the work of scholars who tested Galanter's thesis outside the American setting.

2. Italics in original.

3. In recent decades China has focused on a "rule-of-law" project, according to Gallagher (2006), in which "reliance on the legal system and a concerted attempt to replace mass campaigns and administrative rule with some kind of 'rule of law' has been a hallmark of China's reforms since the early 1980s" (785). As we note throughout this chapter, the preferred status of repeat players may shift over time.

4. Ipsen (2020) also compares the Chilean case study with a firm located in Hawaii and finds similar use of legal strategies to prevail.

5. Chodosh, May, and Singhvi (1997–98) also find that delays can benefit the haves in their study of the Indian civil justice system.

6. Collins and McCarthy (2017) study the participation of interest groups before the high courts of eleven countries from 1969 to 2002 and find that participation as intervenor or as amicus curiae increases when courts have the power of judicial review and articulated rights.

3. Winners and Losers

1. The case is *Hunter and others v. Canary Wharf Ltd* [1997] 2 All ER 426.

2. The case is *Buckley J in Bridlington Relay Ltd v. Yorkshire Electricity Board* [1965] 1 All ER 264.

3. The decision was *Chastey v. Ackland* [1895] 2 Ch 389.

4. See *Thompson-Schwab v. Costaki* ([1956] 1 WLR 335).

5. Staff, "The Fall of Derry Irvine," *Scotsman,* August 19, 2004, https://www.scotsman.com/arts-and-culture/fall-derry-irvine-2463956; Michael White, "Why Tony and Cherie Love 'Cupid QC,'" *Guardian,* February 20, 2011, https://www.theguardian.com/politics/2001/feb/20/uk.labour4.

6. *Johnson v. American Home Assurance Company* [1998] HCA 14; 192 CLR 266; ALR 162; 72 ALJR 610 (4 March 1998).

7. The data are derived from the National High Courts Database, the compilation of which was funded by the National Science Foundation under grants SES No. 9975237 (2000) and SES No. 0137055 (2002–2006). See appendix A for the selection criteria for the countries included in the data set.

8. In an attempt to be consistent with the earlier work of McCormick (1993) and Songer and Sheehan (1992), all "boards and agencies established by and operating under the authority of the respective levels of government, as well as ministers and agency heads acting in their official capacity," were included in each government category (McCormick 1993, 527). Litigants were classified as individuals only if it appeared that they were neither government officials nor officers or owners of businesses. For example, if a litigant was listed only by name in the title of the case, but it was apparent from the opinion that this litigant was the owner of an auto repair shop

who was being sued for defective repair work the shop had performed, the litigant
would be coded as a business.

9. The national and subnational governments are combined for these analyses.

4. Examining the Success of the Government Gorilla

1. The case is *State of Karnataka v. Moorthy Alias B. Moorthy* (1983) 3 SCC 268.

2. Section 50 of the Electricity Act of 1910.

3. Notification No. KEB/A5/6053/73–74/SOL/401/72, dated 18 April 1974, making
the authorization appeared in the *Karnataka Electricity Board Manual*, vol. 1, 2nd
ed., p. 80.

4. The High Court is the supreme judicial body in each state.

5. All bills, acts, rules, notifications, orders, and so forth of the government of India are
officially made public through publication in the *Gazette of India*.

6. *Ram Chander Prasad Sharma v. State of Bihar* AIR 1967 SC 349; *Vishwanath v. Emperor* AIR 1936 All 742; *State (Delhi Administration) v. Dharam Pal* 1980 Cri LJ 1394;
Balkrishna Anant Hirlekar v. Emperor AIR 1931 Bom 132.

7. *State of Karnataka v. Abdul Nabi* 1975 Cri LJ 746.

8. *State of Karnataka v. Moorthy Alias B. Moorthy* (1983) 3 SCC 271.

9. The court held that the internal notice and publication in the manual satisfied the
"notification" requirement. Moreover, the court recognized that official publication
in the *Gazette* was appropriately required under section 16 of the Criminal Law
Amendment Act of 1908 for those crimes that could limit "the rights and liberties of
the citizens" ((1983) 3 SCC 274). Mr. Moorthy faced no such penalty.

10. *Panotes v. Employees' Compensation Commission, Government Service Insurance System
(Ministry of Education and Culture)* G. R. No. L-64802, March 29, 1984.

11. *Panotes v. Employees' Compensation Commission, Government Service Insurance System
(Ministry of Education and Culture)* (1985) 138 SCRA 602.

12. *Panotes v. Employees' Compensation Commission, Government Service Insurance System
(Ministry of Education and Culture)* (1985) 138 SCRA 610–11.

13. *Panotes v. Employees' Compensation Commission, Government Service Insurance System
(Ministry of Education and Culture)* G. R. No. L-64802, March 29, 1984.

14. *Panotes v. Employees' Compensation Commission, Government Service Insurance System
(Ministry of Education and Culture)* G. R. No. L-64802, March 29, 1984.

15. *Panotes v. Employees' Compensation Commission, Government Service Insurance System
(Ministry of Education and Culture)* (1985) 138 SCRA 606.

5. A Comparative Analysis of Party Capability Theory

1. Owing to the lack of transparency during the states of emergency, the exact number
of detainees is not known, but civil rights groups estimate that more than 30,000
people were detained following the June 12, 1986, declaration of a state of emergency
and the subsequent extensions of it (Merrett 1990). Bennett and Quinn (1988)
report 20,000 detainees for 1986 alone. Official figures of detainees under the 1985
emergency put the number at 7,966 (see House of Assembly Debates, March 27,
1985, col. 2827). No further official numbers were provided for subsequent emer-

gency orders. Other estimates note the total number of detentions as high as 45,000, with over 4,000 deaths (van Zyl Slabbert 1989).

2. Van Zyl Slabbert (1989, 7) documents over 4,012 deaths due to civil unrest, 45,000 detentions, and 1,148 work stoppages from 1984 to 1987. Insurgent actions by the African National Congress rose from 44 in 1984 to 203 in 1986 and there were over 1,000 work stoppages and strikes by 1987, all of which led to a "virtual breakdown of and rebellion against" apartheid structures.

3. On property ownership, see the 1936 Bantu Trust and Land Act and the 1945 Bantu Urban Areas Consolidation Act, as well as subsequent variations on the theme that regulated where and why Black South Africans would be allowed to live within the republic. On love, see the 1950 Immorality Amendment Act. On marriage, see the Prohibition of Mixed Marriages Act of 1949. On speech, see section 118 of the Defense Act (Act 44 of 1957), which allowed essentially unfettered banning of publications and films, and the Publications Act (Act 42 of 1974). For a full description of the arsenal of acts used to limit freedom of expression, see Marcus (1992b), "Freedom of Expression and National Security: The South African Experience," and Mathews's (1972) extensive catalogue in *Law, Order and Liberty in South Africa,* both of which were critical sources for this section. With respect to freedom of association and assembly, the Suppression of Communism Act of 1950 and the Internal Security Act (Act 74 of 1982) could prohibit any gatherings that lacked official approval, confine individuals to particular areas, and prohibit individuals from being quoted, among many other restrictions.

4. The statute was passed in response to the Defiance Campaign of 1952 led by Nelson Mandela and others and allowed the governor-general (which became the state president subsequently) to declare a state of emergency in any or every part of the country and rule by proclamation.

5. Also passed in response to the Defiance Campaign, the statute prohibited individuals from "protesting against the law" (section 2b) themselves or in any way advising, encouraging, or aiding others to do so. This statue and the Public Safety Act together criminalized peaceful protest, leaving only violence to replace it.

6. Not only does the act declare the Communist Party of South Africa an unlawful organization, the state president could similarly declare any organization unlawful if the president is satisfied (and the president alone is judge and jury, though technically the president receives the advice of the Executive Council) that the organization promotes communism or any of the tenets of communism.

7. Act 17 of 1956 was a revision of its 1914 predecessor that allowed the minister of justice to prohibit public gatherings, publications, or conduct that could engender "feelings of hostility" (chapter I, section 2 (3)). It also included language so broad and vague as to cast an inexhaustibly wide net. Under section 10 any person in a public place who behaved in an "offensive manner by jeers, jibes or like conduct" (chapter II, section 10 (d)) could be punished and the onus to prove innocence was placed on the accused.

8. Following the Sharpeville uprising, parliament passed the Unlawful Organizations Act (Act 34 of 1960) banning the primary political opposition groups, the African

National Congress and the Pan-African Congress. Individuals "listed" as members or even associates of these groups could not engage in any activities deemed to further the aim of the banned organizations.

9. Formally the General Law Amendment Act (Act 76 of 1962), the statute provided a broad definition of sabotage from serious threats to public safety, such as endangering the water supply, to fairly innocuous damage, even minimal, to property. The onus to prove innocence rested on the accused and the penalties ranged from a mandatory minimum of five years to death.

10. Formally the General Law Amendment Act (Act 37 of 1963), the statute authorized detention without trial for up to ninety days in solitary confinement. Any police officer could arrest without warrant any individual whom the officer suspected on reasonable grounds to have committed any offense under the Suppression of Communism Act, the Unlawful Organizations Act, or generally considered needed for interrogation. No one, save a magistrate, who was required to visit weekly, could have access to any detainee without the consent of the minister of justice.

11. The Criminal Procedure Amendment Act (Act 96 of 1965) doubled down (literally) on the ability to detain, extending the time to 180 days.

12. Act 83 of 1967 was a companion to the Sabotage Act and equally broad in its description of offenses, which included any action that would "embarrass the administration of the affairs of the State" (section 2.2.l). Yet again, the onus to prove innocence fell on the accused, and the penalties equaled that of treason and paralleled those of the Sabotage Act, which included a mandatory minimum of five years and up to the death penalty.

13. Act 51 of 1968 was theoretically passed to prohibit one racial group from interfering with the politics of another racial group. The law made it a crime for racial groups to coalesce, including multiple racial groups joining a political party or even one racial group supporting the political party of another racial group. This emerged in 1966 in response to the Progressive Party admitting persons of all races as members. Its growing success presented a growing threat (Matthews 1972, 206–8).

14. As Marcus notes, the Internal Security Act (Act 74 of 1982) consolidated the bulk of South Africa's security laws into one statute retaining "most of the obnoxious provisions" of each, including indefinite detention for the purposes of interrogation, preventive detention, and detention of witnesses, along with the prohibition of gatherings and publications, the banning of organizations, and a host of restrictions on individuals (Marcus 1992a, 38).

15. *Omar and Others v. Minister of Law and Order and Other* 1987 (3) 859 AD.

16. The Group Areas Act is Act No. 41 of 1950.

17. Benjamin Pound, "Dullah Omar: Politician of Post-Apartheid South Africa," *London Independent*, March 15, 2004, https://www.independent.co.uk/news/obituaries/dullah-omar-38171.html.

18. These include the Unlawful Organizations Act, the Public Safety Act, the Criminal Law Amendment Act, the Riotous Assemblies Act, and the Sabotage Act, among others.

19. See, e.g., *Loza v. Police Station Commander* 1964 (2) SA 545 (A), *Rossouw v. Sachs* 1964 (2) SA 551 (A), and *Schermbrucker v. Klindt N.O.* 1965 (4) SA 606 (A).
20. For "executive minded," see Cameron (1982).
21. See, e.g., *Komani N.O. v. Bantu Affairs Administration Board, Peninsula Area* (1980 (4) SA 448 (A)) and *Oos-Randse Administrasieraad en 'n ander v. Rikhoto* 1983 (3) SA 595 (A).
22. The judgment in this case is unreported.
23. The case is *Bill v. State President and Others* 1987 (1) SA 265 (W).
24. Under the 1985 and 1986 states of emergency orders, the initial period of detention was fourteen days, after which the minister of law and order could extend it for the full duration of the state of emergency. The 1987 State of Emergency extended the initial detention period to thirty days.
25. *Omar and Others v. Minister of Law and Order and Others* 1986(3) 306 CPD.
26. *Omar and Others v. Minister of Law and Order and Other* 1987(3) 863–864.
27. *Omar and Others v. Minister of Law and Order and Other* 1987(3) 886–888.
28. *Omar and Others v. Minister of Law and Order and Other* 1987(3) 907.
29. *Omar and Others v. Minister of Law and Order and Others* 1987 (1) SA 909 (A).
30. See, e.g., *Sachs v. Minister of Justice* 1934 AD 11: "Parliament may make any encroachment it pleases upon the life, liberty and property of any individual subject to its sway."
31. His father disappeared into German hands very soon after the invasion, while his older sister was deported to Treblinka, where she too ultimately perished (Morton 1992, 30).
32. The decision of the Court of Appeal was considered so offensive that the Canadian Parliament passed the so-called Morgentaler Amendment, altering the Criminal Code of Canada to ensure that courts of appeal cannot overturn jury verdicts but may only order a new trial.
33. *Morgentaler v. the Queen* (1975) 20 C.C.C. (2d).
34. *R. v. Morgentaler* (1988) 1 SCR 30.
35. On India, see Dutt (1976).
36. Our number of 14,500 excludes cases in which the appellant won in part and lost in part.
37. The data set can be found at v-dem.net.
38. We do not include a variable for the ideology of the judges. We are interested in the aggregate outcome of the case and not the individual votes of the justices, but more critically, there is not a common measure of ideology available for all the countries.
39. Because of issues related to perfect collinearity, we cannot include dummy variables in model A for both the national government appearing as the appellant and respondent. Therefore, we only include results for the *National Government as Appellant* since that variable's coefficient is opposite our theoretical expectation. When we run model A with *National Government as Respondent* that variable is significant and positive, as we hypothesize.
40. Because of issues related to perfect collinearity, we cannot include dummy variables in model C for both the national government appearing as the appellant and as

respondent. Therefore we only include results for the *National Government as Respondent.*

41. *R v. Morgentaler* (1988) 1 SCR 32–33.
42. *R v. Morgentaler* (1988) 1 SCR 38.

Appendix A

1. Compilation of the National High Courts Database, from which the data are derived, was funded by the National Science Foundation under grants SES No. 9975237 (2000) and SES No. 0137055 (2002–2006).

REFERENCES

Abel, Richard L. 1995. *Politics by Other Means: Law in the Struggle against Apartheid, 1980–1994.* New York: Routledge.

Aiken, Jane Harris, and Michael Musheno. 1994. "Why Have-Nots Win in the HIV Litigation Arena: Socio-Legal Dynamics of Extreme Cases." *Law and Policy* 16:267–97.

Alarie, Benjamin, and Andrew Green. 2017. *Commitment and Cooperation on High Courts.* New York: Oxford University Press.

Albiston, Catherine. 2003. "The Rule of Law and the Litigation Process: The Paradox of Losing by Winning." In *Litigation: Do the "Haves" Still Come Out Ahead?,* ed. Herbert M. Kritzer and Susan Silbey. Stanford: Stanford University Press.

———. 1999. "The Rule of Law and the Litigation Process: The Paradox of Losing by Winning." *Law and Society Review* 33:869–910.

Albonetti, C. A. 1987. "Prosecutorial Discretion: The Effects of Uncertainty." *Law and Society Review* 21:291–313.

Ashenfelter, Orley, Theodore Eisenberg, and Stewart J. Schwab. 1995. "Politics and the Judiciary: The Influence of Judicial Background on Case Outcomes." *Journal of Legal Studies* 24 (2): 257–81.

Ashford, Kathryn L. 1986. "The Role of Corporations in the 1980 U.S. Congressional Elections." *Sociological Inquiry* 56:409–31.

Atkins, Burton M. 1991. "Party Capability Theory as an Explanation for Intervention Behavior in the English Court of Appeal." *American Journal of Political Science* 35:881–903.

Bagashka, Tanya, and Lydia Brashear Tiede. 2021. "The Influence of Procurator Generals in Constitutional Review." *Journal of Law and Courts* 9 (1): 189–214.

Bailey, Michael A., Brian Kamoie, and Forrest Maltzman. 2005. "Signals from the Tenth Justice: The Political Role of the Solicitor General in Supreme Court Decision Making." *American Journal of Political Science* 49:72–85.

Baker, Tom. 2001. "Blood Money, New Money, and the Moral Economy of Tort Law in Action." *Law and Society Review* 35 (2): 275–319.

Ball, Jeremy D. 2006. "Is It a Prosecutor's World? Determinants of Count Bargaining Decisions." *Journal of Contemporary Criminal Justice* 22:241–60.

Baum, Lawrence. 1977. "Judicial Specialization, Litigant Influence, and Substantive Policy: The Court of Customs and Patent Appeals." *Law and Society Review* 11:823–50.

Beavers, Staci L., and Craig F. Emmert. 2000. "Explaining State High-Courts' Selective Use of State Constitutions." *Publius* 30:1–15.

Bennett, M. and D. Quinn. 1988. *Political Conflict in South Africa: Data Trends 1984–1988.* Indicator Project South Africa, University of Natal, Durban.

Bezdek, Barbara. 1992. "Silence in the Court: Participation and Subordination of Poor Tenants' Voices in Legal Process." *Hofstra Law Review* 20:533–608.

Bingham, Lisa B. 1998. "On Repeat Players, Adhesive Contracts, and the Use of Statistics in Judicial Review of Employment Arbitration Awards." *McGeorge Law Review* 29:223–59.

———. 1997. "Employment Arbitration: The Repeat Player Effect." *Employee Rights and Employment Policy Journal* 1:189–220.

Black, Donald. 1976. *The Behavior of Law*. New York: Academic Press.

Black, Ryan C., and Ryan J. Owens. 2012. *The Solicitor General and the United States Supreme Court: Executive Branch Influence and Judicial Decisions*. New York: Cambridge University Press.

Blankenburg, Erhard. 1994. "The Infrastructure for Avoiding Civil Litigation: Comparing Cultures of Legal Behavior in the Netherlands and West Germany." *Law and Society Review* 28:789–808.

———. 1981–82. "Legal Insurance, Litigant Decisions, and the Rising Caseloads of Courts: A West German Study." *Law and Society Review* 16:601–24.

Boucher, Robert L. Jr., and Jeffrey A. Segal. 1995. "Supreme Court Justices as Strategic Decision-Makers: Aggressive Grants and Defensive Denials on the Vinson Court." *Journal of Politics* 57:812–23.

Boyd, C. 2015. "Litigant Status and Trial Court Appeal Mobilization: Trial Court Appeals." *Law and Policy* 37 (4): 294–323.

Bradt, Andrew D., and D. Theodore Rave. 2019. "It's Good to Have the 'Haves' on Your Side: A Defense of Repeat Players in Multidistrict Litigation." *Georgetown Law Journal* 108:78–123.

Brace, Paul, and Melinda Gann Hall. 2001. "'Haves' versus 'Have Nots' in State Supreme Courts: Allocating Docket Space and Wins in Power Asymmetric Cases." *Law and Society Review* 35:393–417.

———. 1997. "The Interplay of Preferences, Case Facts, Context, and Rules in the Politics of Judicial Choice." *Journal of Politics* 59:1206–31.

———. 1993. "Integrated Models of Judicial Dissent." *Journal of Politics* 55:914–35.

———. 1990. "Neoinstitutionalism and Dissent in State Supreme Courts." *Journal of Politics* 52:54–70.

Brenner, Saul, and Marc Stier. 1996. "Retesting Segal and Spaeth's Stare Decisis Model." *American Journal of Political Science* 40:1035–48.

Brisbin, Richard Jr. 1996. "Slaying the Dragon: Segal, Spaeth and the Function of Law in Supreme Court Decision Making." *American Journal of Political Science* 40: 1004–17.

Brown, Charles A. 2011. "Employment Discrimination Plaintiffs in the District of Maryland." *Cornell Law Review* 96:1247–71.

Browne, William P. 1990. "Organized Interests and Their Issue Niches: A Search for Pluralism in a Policy Domain." *Journal of Politics* 52 (2): 477–509.

Bruff, Harold H. 1973. "Arizona's Inferior Courts." *Law and the Social Order* 1:1–48.

Bruijn, M., and M. Vols. 2020. "Upperdogs versus Underdogs: Judicial Review of Administrative Drug-Related Closures in the Netherlands." *Recht Der Werkelijkhid* 41 (1): 25–49.

Burch, Elizabeth C. 2017. "Monopolies in Multidistrict Litigation." *Vanderbilt Law Review* 70:67–166.

Burch, Elizabeth C., and Margaret S. Williams. 2017. "Repeat Players in Multidistrict Litigation: The Social Network." *Cornell Law Review* 102:1445–63.

Cameron, Edwin. 1982. "Legal Chauvinism, Executive-Mindedness and Justice—L. C. Steyn's Impact on South African Law." *South African Law Journal* 99:38–75.

Camp Keith, Linda. 2002. "Constitutional Provisions for Individual Human Rights (1976–1996): Are They More Than Mere 'Window Dressing'?" *Political Research Quarterly* 55:111–43.

Camp Keith, Linda, C. Neal Tate, and Steven C. Poe "Is the Law a Mere Parchment Barrier to Human Rights Abuse?" *Journal of Politics* 71 (22): 644–60.

Canon, Bradley C., and Michael Giles. 1972. "Recurring Litigants: Federal Agencies before the Supreme Court." *Western Political Quarterly* 25:183–91.

Cardozo, Benjamin N. 1921. *The Nature of the Judicial Process*. New Haven: Yale University Press.

Carp, Robert, and C. K. Rowland. 1983. *Policy Making and Politics in the Federal District Courts*. Knoxville: University of Tennessee Press.

Cartwright, Bliss. 1975. "Conclusion: Disputes and Reported Cases." *Law and Society Review* 9 (2): 369–84.

Castelliano de Vasconcelos, Caio, Eduardo Wantanabe, and Waldir Leoncio Netto. 2018. "The Impact of Attorneys on Judicial Decisions: Empirical Evidence from Civil Cases." *International Journal for Court Administration* 9 (2): 32–42.

Chan, P. 2019. "Do the Haves Come Out Ahead in Chinese Grassroots Courts: Rural Land Disputes between Married-out Women and Village Collectives." *Hastings Law Journal* 71:1.

Chandrasekher, A., and D. Horton. 2019. "Arbitration Nation: Data from Four Providers." *California Law Review* 107:1.

Cheit, Ross E., and Jacob E. Gersen. 2000. "When Businesses Sue Each Other: An Empirical Study of State Court Litigation." *Law and Social Inquiry* 25:789–816.

Chen, K.-P, K.-C. Huang, and C.-C. Lin. 2014. "Party Capability versus Court Preference: Why Do the 'Haves' Come Out Ahead? An Empirical Lesson from the Taiwan Supreme Court." *Journal of Law, Economics, and Organizations* 31 (1): 93–126.

Chin, Audrey, and Mark Peterson. 1985. *Deep Pockets, Empty Pockets: Who Wins in Cook County Jury Trials*. Santa Monica, CA: Rand.

Chodosh, Hiram E., Stephen A. Mayo, A. M. Ahmadi, and Abhishek M. Singhvi. 1997–98. "Indian Civil Justice System Reform: Limitation and Preservation of the Adversarial Process." *Journal of International Law and Politics* 30:1–78.

Clawson, Dan, Alan Neustadtl and Denise Scott. 1992. *Money Talks: Corporate PACs and Political Influence*. New York: Basic Books.

Cohen, M. R. 1914. "The Process of Judicial Legislation." *American Law Review* 68:161–98.

Collins, Paul M. 2004. "Friends of the Court: Examining the Influence of Amicus Curiae Participation in U.S. Supreme Court Litigation." *Law and Society Review* 38 (4): 807–32.

Collins, Paul M., and Lauren A. McCarthy. 2017. "Friends and Interveners: Interest Group Litigation in a Comparative Context." *Journal of Law and Courts* 5 (1): 55–80.

Colvin, A. 2011. "An Empirical Study of Employment Arbitration: Case Outcomes and Processes." *Journal of Empirical Legal Studies* 8 (1): 1–23.

Colvin, A., and M. Gough. 2015. "Individual Employment Rights Arbitration in the

United States: Actors and Outcomes." *Industrial and Labor Relations Review* 68 (5): 1019–42.

Conti, J. 2010. "Learning to Dispute: Repeat Participation, Expertise, and Reputation at the World Trade Organization." *Law and Social Inquiry* 35 (3): 625–62.

Coppedge, Michael, John Gerring, Staffan I. Lindberg, Svend-Erik Skaaning, Jan Toerell, Joshua Krusell, Valeriya Mechkova, Josefine Perne, Moa Olin, Laura Saxer, Natalia Stepanova, and Johannes Roemer. 2017. "V-Dem Organization and Management." Available at www.v-dem.net.

Corder, Hugh, and Dennis Davis. 1989. "The Constitutional Guidelines of the African National Congress: A Preliminary Assessment." *South African Law Journal* 106:642–47.

Coughlin, Cletus G. 1985. "Domestic Content Legislation: House Voting and the Economic Theory of Regulation." *Economic Inquiry* 23:437–48.

Crowley, Donald W. 1987. "Judicial Review of Administrative Agencies: Does the Type of Agency Matter?" *Western Political Quarterly* 40:265–83.

Curry, T. 2015. A Look at the Bureaucratic Nature of the Office of the Solicitor General. *Justice System Journal* 36 (2): 180–91.

Daly, Kathleen, and Michael Tonry. 1997. "Gender, Race, and Sentencing." *Crime and Justice* 22:201–52.

Davies, Thomas Y. 1982. "Affirmed: A Study of Criminal Appeals and Decision-Making Norms in a California Court of Appeal." *American Bar Foundation Research Journal* 3:543–648.

Denzau, Arthur T., and Michael Munger. 1986. "Legislators and Interest Groups: How Unorganized Interests Get Represented." *American Political Science Review.* 80 (1): 89–106.

Dhavan, Rajeev. 1985. "Judging the Judges." In *Judges and the Judicial Power,* ed. Rajeev Dhavan, R. Sudarshan, and Salman Khurshid. London: Sweet & Maxwell.

Dickens, Charles. 1839. *Nicholas Nickleby.* London: Chapman & Hall.

Dixon, Jo. 1995. "The Organizational Context of Criminal Sentencing." *American Journal of Sociology* 100 (5): 1157–98.

Dotan, Yoav. 1999a. "Judicial Rhetoric, Government Lawyers, and Human Rights: The Case of the Israeli High Court of Justice during the Intafada." *Law and Society Review* 33:319–63.

———. 1999b. "Do the 'Haves' Still Come out Ahead? Resource Inequalities in Ideological Courts: The Case of the Israeli High Court of Justice." *Law and Society Review* 33:1059–80.

Dugard, John. 1978. *Human Rights in the South African Legal Order.* Princeton, NJ: Princeton University Press.

Dumas, Tao L. and Stacia L. Haynie. 2012. "Building an Integrated Model of Trial Court Decision-Making: Predicting Plaintiff Success and Awards across Circuits." *State Politics and Policy Quarterly* 12:103–26.

Dumas, Tao L., Stacia L. Haynie, and Dorothy Daboval. 2015. "Does Size Matter? The Influence of Law Firm Size on Litigant Success Rates." *Justice System Journal* 36:341–54.

Dunworth, Terence, and Joel Rogers. 1996. "Corporations in Court: Big Business Litigation in U.S. Federal Courts, 1971–1991." *Law and Social Inquiry* 21:497–592.

Dutt, V. P. 1976. "The Emergency in India: Background and Rationale." *Asian Survey* 16:1124–38.

Dyzenhaus, David. 1998. *Hard Cases in Wicked Legal Systems: Pathologies of Legality.* New York: Oxford University Press.

Dzmitryieva, A., K. Titaev, and I. Chetverikova. 2016. "The State and Business at Arbitrazh Courts." *Russian Politics and Law* 54:281–311.

Easton, David. 1965. *A Framework for Political Analysis.* Englewood Cliffs, NJ: Prentice-Hall.

Edelman, Lauren B., Linda H. Krieger, Scott R. Eliason, Catherine R. Albiston, and Virginia Mellema. 2011. "When Organizations Rule: Judicial Deference to Institutionalized Employment Structures." *American Journal of Sociology* 117:888–954.

Edelman, Lauren B., and Mark C. Suchman. 2003. "When the 'Haves' Hold Court: Speculations on the Organizational Internalization of Law." In *In Litigation: Do the "Haves" Still Come Out Ahead?*, ed. Herbert M. Kritzer and Susan Silbey. Stanford: Stanford University Press.

———. 1999. "When the 'Haves' Hold Court: Speculations on the Organizational Internalization of Law." *Law and Society Review* 33:941–91.

Edelman, Lauren B., Linda H. Krieger, Scott R. Eliason, Catherine R. Albiston, and Virginia Mellema. 2011. "When Organizations Rule: Judicial Deference to Institutionalized Employment Structures." *American Journal of Sociology* 117:888–954.

Eisenberg, Theodore, and Henry Farber. 2003. "The Government as Litigant: Further Tests of the Case Selection Model." *American Law and Economics Review* 5:94–133.

———. 1997. "The Litigious Plaintiff Hypothesis: Case Selection and Resolution." *Rand Journal of Economics* 28:S92–S112.

Eisenberg, Theodore, Talia Fisher, and Issi Rosen. 2011. "Israel's Supreme Court Appellate Jurisdiction: An Empirical Study." *Cornell Law Review* 96:693–725.

Ellman, Stephen. 1992. *In a Time of Trouble: Law and Liberty in South Africa's State of Emergency.* New York: Oxford University Press.

Emmert, Craig. 1991. "Litigants in State Supreme Court Judicial Review Cases: Participation and Success." *Justice System Journal* 14:486–93.

Epstein, Lee. 1985. *Conservatives in Court.* Knoxville: University of Tennessee Press.

Epstein, Lee, and C. K. Rowland. 1991. "Debunking the Myth of Interest Group Invincibility in the Courts." *American Political Science Review* 85:205–17.

Fainstein, Susan S. 1994. *The City Builders: Property, Politics, and Planning in London and New York.* Cambridge, MA: Blackwell.

Farole, Donald J. 1999. "Reexamining Litigant Success in State Supreme Courts." *Law and Society Review* 33:1043–58.

Feldstein, Paul J., and Glenn Melnick. 1984. "Congressional Voting Behavior on Hospital Legislation: An Exploratory Study." *Journal of Health Politics, Policy, and Law* 8:686–701.

Feuille, Peter. 1997. "Dispute Resolution Frontiers in the Unionized Workplace." In

Workplace Dispute Resolution: Directions for the Twenty-First Century, ed. Sandra E. Gleason. East Lansing: Michigan State University Press.

Flemming, Roy B., and Glen S. Krutz. 2002a. "Selecting Appeals for Judicial Review in Canada: A Replication and Multivariate Test of American Hypotheses." *Journal of Politics* 64:232–48.

———. 2002b. "Repeat Litigators and Agenda Setting on the Supreme Court of Canada." *Canadian Journal of Political Science* 35:811–33.

Frank, Jerome. 1930. *Law and the Modern Mind.* New York: Doubleday.

Friedman, Lawrence M. 1989. "Litigation and Society." *Annual Review of Sociology* 15: 17–29.

Galanter, Marc. 1975. "Afterword: Explaining Litigation." *Law and Society Review* 9: 347–68.

———. 1974. "Why the 'Haves' Come Out Ahead: Speculation on the Limits of Legal Change." *Law and Society Review* 9 (1): 95–160.

Gallagher, Mary E. 2006. "Mobilizing the Law in China: 'Informed Disenchantment' and the Development of Legal Consciousness." *Law and Society Review* 40:783–816.

Gazal-Ayal, O., and R. Perry. 2014. "Imbalances of Power in ADR: The Impact of Representation and Dispute Resolution Method on Case Outcomes." *Law and Social Inquiry* 39:791–823.

George, Tracey E., and Lee Epstein. 1992. "On the Nature of Supreme Court Decision Making." *American Political Science Review* 86:323–37.

Gibson, James L., and Michael J. Nelson. 2021. *Judging Inequality: State Supreme Courts and the Inequality Crisis.* New York: Russell Sage Foundation.

Gilad, S. 2010. "Why the 'Haves' do not Necessarily Come Out Ahead in Informal Dispute Resolution." *Law and Policy* 32:283–312.

Gray, Virginia, and David Lowery. 1995. "Interest Representation and Democratic Gridlock." *Legislative Studies Quarterly* 20 (4): 531–52.

Gross, Samuel R. 1996. "Don't Try: Civil Jury Verdicts in a System Geared to Settlement." *UCLA Law Review* 44:1–64.

Grossman, Joel B., Herbert M. Kritzer, and Stewart Macaulay. 1999. "Do the 'Haves' Still Come Out Ahead?." *Law and Society Review* 33:803–10.

Grossman, Joel B., and Austin Sarat. 1975. "Litigation in the Federal Courts: A Comparative Perspective." *Law and Society Review* 75:321–46.

Gujarati, Damodar N. 2003. *Basic Econometrics,* ed. 4 Boston: McGraw-Hill.

Hadfield, Gillian K. 2005. "Exploring Economic and Democratic Theories of Civil Litigation: Differences between Individual and Organizational Litigants in the Disposition of Federal Civil Cases." *Stanford Law Review* 57:1275–327.

Hagan, John. 1982. "The Corporate Advantage: A Study of the Involvement of Corporate and Individual Victims in a Criminal Justice System." *Social Forces* 60:993–1022.

Haire, Susan B., Stefanie A. Lindquist, and Roger Hartley. 1999. "Attorney Expertise, Litigant Success, and Judicial Decision Making in the U.S. Courts of Appeals." *Law and Society Review* 33:667–85.

Haire, Susan B., and Laura P. Moyer. 2008. "Advocacy through Briefs in the US Courts of Appeals." *Southern Illinois University Law Journal* 32:593–609.

Haire, Susan B., Stefanie Lindquist, and Donald Songer. 2003. "Appellate Court Supervision in the Federal Judiciary: A Hierarchical Perspective." *Law and Society Review* 37:143–67.

Hakman, Nathan. 1966. "Lobbying the Supreme Court—An Appraisal of Political Science Folklore." *Fordham Law Review* 35:15–50.

Hall, Melinda Gann. 1987. "Constituent Influence in State Supreme Courts: Conceptual Notes and a Case Study." *Journal of Politics* 49:1117–26.

Hamzehzadeh, Bahaar. 2010. "Repeat Player vs. One-Shotter: Is Victory All That Obvious?" *Hastings Business Law Journal* 6:239–59.

Hanretty, C. 2020. *A Court of Specialists: Judicial Behavior on the UK Supreme Court.* New York: Oxford University Press.

Hanretty, C. 2014. "Haves and Have-Nots before the Law Lords." *Political Studies* 62:686–97.

Harris, Beth. 2003. "Representing Homeless Families: Repeat Player Implementation Strategies." In *In Litigation: Do the "Haves" Still Come Out Ahead?*, ed. Herbert M. Kritzer and Susan Silbey. Stanford: Stanford University Press.

———. 1999. "Representing Homeless Families: Repeat Player Implementation Strategies." *Law and Society Review* 33:911–39.

Harris, Catherine T., Ralph Peeples, and Thomas B. Metzloff. 2008. "Does Being a Repeat Player Make a Difference? The Impact of Attorney Experience and Case-Picking on the Outcome of Medical Malpractice Lawsuits." *Yale Journal of Health Policy, Law, and Ethics* 8:253–82.

———. 2005. "Who Are Those Guys? An Empirical Examination of Medical Malpractice Plaintiffs' Attorneys." *SMU Law Review* 58:225–50.

Haynie, Stacia L. 2004. "Structure and Context of Judicial Institutions in Democratizing Countries: The Philippines and South Africa." *Arellano Law and Policy Review* 5:25–56.

———. 2003. *Judging in Black and White: Decision Making in the South African Appellate Division, 1950–1990.* New York: Peter Lang.

———. 1995. "Resource Inequalities and Regional Variation in Litigation Outcomes in the Philippine Supreme Court, 1961–1986." *Political Research Quarterly* 48:371–80.

———. 1994. "Resource Inequalities and Litigation Outcomes in the Philippine Supreme Court." *Journal of Politics* 56:752–72.

Haynie, Stacia L., and Kaitlyn L. Sill. 2007. "Experienced Advocates and Litigation Outcomes: Repeat Players in the South African Supreme Court of Appeal." *Political Research Quarterly* 60:443–53.

Hazelton, Morgan L. W., and Rachael K. Hinkle. 2022. *Persuading the Supreme Court: The Significance of Briefs in Judicial Decision Making.* Lawrence: University Press of Kansas.

He, Xin, and Fen Lin. 2017. "The Losing Media? An Empirical Study of Defamation Litigation in China." *China Quarterly* 230:371–98.

He, X[in], and Y. Su. 2013. "Do the 'Haves' Come Out Ahead in Shanghai Courts?" *Journal of Empirical Legal Studies* 10:120–45.

Heinz, John, and Edward Laumann. 1982. *Chicago Lawyers: The Social Structure of the Bar.* New York: Russell Sage Foundation.

Heinz, John P., Edward O. Laumann, Robert L. Nelson, and Robert H. Salisbury. 1993. *The Hollow Core: Private Interests in National Policy Making.* Cambridge, MA: Harvard University Press.

Helmke, Gretchen. 2005. *Courts under Constraints: Judges, Generals, and Presidents in Argentina.* New York: Cambridge University Press.

———. 2003. "Checks and Balances by Other Means: Strategic Defection and the 'Re-Reelection' Controversy in Argentina." *Comparative Politics* 35 (2): 213–28.

Henderson, James, and Theodore Eisenberg. 1990. "The Quiet Revolution in Products Liability: An Empirical Study of Legal Change." *UCLA Law Review* 37:479–553.

Hendley, Kathryn, Peter Murrell, and Randi Ryterman. 2003. "Do Repeat Players Behave Differently in Russia? Contractual and Litigation Behavior of Russian Enterprises." In *In Litigation: Do the "Haves" Still Come Out Ahead?*, ed. Herbert M. Kritzer and Susan Silbey. Stanford: Stanford University Press.

———. 1999. "Do Repeat Players Behave Differently in Russia? Contractual and Litigation Behavior of Russian Enterprises." *Law and Society Review* 33:833–67.

Hoffmann, Elizabeth. 2008. "The 'Haves' and 'Have-Nots' within the Organization." *Law and Contemporary Problems* 71:53–64.

Hollingsworth, Robert J., William B. Feldman, and David C. Clark. 1974. "The Ohio Small Claims Court: An Empirical Study." *University of Cincinnati Law Review* 42:469–527.

Horton, D., and A. Chandrasekher. 2016. "Employment Arbitration after the Revolution." *DePaul Law Review* 65:457–96.

———. 2015. "After the Revolution: An Empirical Study of Consumer Arbitration." *Georgetown Law Journal* 104 (1): 57–124.

Howard, R. M. 2001. "Wealth, Power, and the Internet Revenue Service: Changing IRS Audit Policy through Litigation." *Social Science Quarterly* 82:268–80.

Hylton, Keith N. 1993. "Asymmetric Information and the Selection of Disputes for Litigation." *Journal of legal Studies* 22 (1): 187–210.

Ipsen, Annabel. 2020. "Repeat Players, the Law, and Social Change: Redefining the Boundaries of Environmental and Labor Governance through Preemptive and Authoritarian Legality." *Law and Society Review* 54 (1): 201–32.

Johnson, Susan W., and Donald R. Songer. 2002. "The Influence of Presidential versus Home State Senatorial Preferences on the Policy Output of Judges on the United States District Courts." *Law and Society Review* 36:657–76.

Jones, Melissa Lin. 2021. "One-Shotters or Have-Nots Should Come Out Ahead in the District of Columbia's Private Sector Workers' Compensation System, but Do They?" *Journal of the National Association of Administrative Law Judiciary* 41 (1): 1–23.

Jones, Woodrow Jr., and K. Robert Keiser. 1987. "Issue Visibility and the Effects of PAC Money." *Social Science Quarterly* 68:170–76.

Kaheny, Erin B., John T. Szmer, and Tammy A. Sarver. 2011. "Women Lawyers before the Supreme Court of Canada." *Canadian Journal of Political Science* 44 (1): 83–109.

Kau, James B., and Paul H. Rubin. 1981. "The Impact of Labor Unions on the Passage of Economic Legislation." *Journal of Labor Research* 2:133–45.

Kearney, Richard C., and Reginald S. Sheehan. 1992. "Supreme Court Decision Making:

The Impact of Court Composition on State and Local Government Litigation." *Journal of Politics* 4:1008–25.

Kessler, Mark. 1990. "Legal Mobilization for Social Reform: Power and the Politics of Agenda Setting." *Law and Society Review* 24:121–44.

Kidder, Robert L., and Setsuo Miyazawa. 1993. "Long-Term Strategies in Japanese Environmental Litigation." *Law and Social Inquiry* 18:605–27.

Kim, Jieun, Rachel E. Stern, Benjamin L. Liebman, and Xiaohan Wu. 2021. "Closing Open Government: Grassroots Policy Conversion of China's Open Government Information Regulation and Its Aftermath." *Comparative Political Studies* 55:319–47.

Kinsey, Karyl, and Loretta J. Stalans. 2003. "Which 'Haves' Come out Ahead and Why? Cultural Capital and Legal Mobilization in Frontline Law." In *In Litigation: Do the "Haves" Still Come Out Ahead?*, ed. Herbert M. Kritzer and Susan Silbey. Stanford: Stanford University Press.

———. 1999. "Which 'Haves' Come Out Ahead and Why? Cultural Capital and Legal Mobilization in Frontline Law." *Law and Society Review* 33:993–1023.

Knight, Jack, and Lee Epstein. 1996. "The Norm of Stare Decisis." *American Journal of Political Science* 40:1018–35.

Kopczynski, Mary. 2008. "The Haves Coming Out Behind: Galanter's Theory Tested on the WTO Dispute Settlement System." *Asper Review of International Business and Trade Law* 8:25–50.

Kritzer, Herbert M. 2003. "The Government Gorilla: Why Does Government Come Out Ahead in Appellate Courts?" In *In Litigation: Do the "Haves" Still Come Out Ahead?*, ed. Herbert M. Kritzer and Susan Silbey. Stanford: Stanford University Press.

———. 1998. *Legal Advocacy: Lawyers and Non-lawyers at Work*. Ann Arbor: University of Michigan Press.

Krohl, John, and Saul Brenner. 1990. "Strategies in Certiorari Voting in the United States Supreme Court: A Reevaluation." *Western Political Quarterly* 43:335.

Langbein, Laura I. 1986. "Money and Access: Some Empirical Evidence." *Journal of Politics* 48:1052–62.

Laswell, Harold. 1958. *Who Gets What, When and How*. New York: New World Publishing.

Lederman, Leandra. 2006. "Do Attorneys Do Their Clients Justice? An Empirical Study of Lawyers' Effects on Tax Court Litigation Outcomes." *Wake Forest Law Review* 41 (4): 1235–95.

Lempert, Robert O. 1976. "Mobilizing Private Law: An Introductory Essay." *Law and Society Review* 11 (2):173–89.

Lindquist, Stefanie A., Wendy L. Martinek, and Virginia A. Hettinger. 2007. "Splitting the Difference: Modeling Appellate Court Decisions with Mixed Outcomes." *Law and Society Review* 41:429–55.

Linzer, Drew A., and Jeffrey K. Staton. 2015. "A Global Measure of Judicial Independence, 1948–2012." *Journal of Law and Courts* Fall:223–54.

Lizotte, Alan J. 1978. "Extra-Legal Factors in Chicago's Criminal Courts: Testing the Conflict Model of Criminal Justice." *Social Problems* 25:564–80.

Llewellyn, Karl. 1931. "Some Realism About Realism—Responding to Dean Pound." *Harvard Law Review* 44:1222–64.

Lochner, Todd, Ellen Sljan, Walker Davis, Benjamin Bardman, and Rafael Swit. 2020. "Calculating, Credible, or Both? Third-Party Monitors and Repeat Players in Federal Campaign Finance Enforcement." *Election Law Journal: Rules, Politics and Policy* 20 (2): 178–97.

Lu, H., H. Pan, and C. Zhang. 2015. "Political Connectedness and Court Outcomes: Evidence from Chinese Corporate Lawsuits." *Journal of Law and Economics* 58:829–61.

Lundholm, M. 2021. "Compensation and Socio-Economic Status of Borrowers in Foreclosure: Evidence from Swedish Micro-data." *Journal of Consumer Policy* 44:95–116.

Manning, S., and K. Randazzo. 2009. "Leveling the Playing Field? Litigant Success Rates in Health-Care Policy Cases in the US Courts of Appeals." *Justice System Journal* 30:245–53.

Marcus, Gilbert. 1992a. "Civil Liberties under Emergency Rule." In *The Last Years of Apartheid: Civil Liberties in South Africa*, ed. John Dugard, Nicholas Haysom, and Gilbert Marcus. New York: Ford Foundation.

———. 1992b. "Freedom of Expression and National Security: The South African Experience." In *Secrecy and Liberty: National Security, Freedom of Expression and Access to Information*, ed. Sandra Caliber, Paul Hoffman, Joan Fitzpatrick, and Stephen Bowen. The Hague: Martinus Nijhoff.

Martin, Sheilah L. 2002. "Abortion Litigation." In *Women's Legal Strategies in Canada*, ed. Radha Jhappan. Toronto: University of Toronto Press.

Mather, Lynn. 1998. "Theorizing about Trial Courts: Lawyers, Policymaking, and Tobacco Litigation." *Law and Social Inquiry* 23:897–940.

Mathews, A. S. 1972. *Law, Order and Liberty in South Africa*. Berkeley: University of California Press.

McAtee, Andrea, and Kevin T. McGuire. 2007. "Lawyers, Justices, and Issue Salience: When and How Do Legal Arguments Affect the U.S. Supreme Court?" *Law and Society Review* 41:259–78.

McCormick, Peter. 1993. "Party Capability Theory and Appellate Success in the Supreme Court of Canada, 1949–1992." *Journal of Politics* 26:523–40.

McGuire, Kevin T. 1998. "Explaining Executive Success in the U. S. Supreme Court." *Political Research Quarterly* 51:505–26.

———. 1995. "Repeat Players in the Supreme Court: The Role of Experienced Lawyers in Litigation Success." *Journal of Politics* 57:187–96.

McGuire, Kevin T., and Gregory A. Caldeira. 1993. "Lawyers, Organized Interests, and the Law of Obscenity: Agenda Setting in the Supreme Court." *American Political Science Review* 87:715–26.

McIntosh, Wayne. 1985. "A State Court's Clientele: Exploring the Strategy of Trial Litigation." *Law and Society Review* 19:421–48.

———. 1980–81. "150 Years of Litigation and Dispute Settlement: A Court Tale." *Law and Society Review* 15:823–48.

McKie, Craig, and Paul Reed. 1981. "Women in Canadian Civil Courts." *Canadian Journal of Sociology* 6:485–504.

Meeker, James W. 1984. "Criminal Appeals over the Last 100 Years: Are the Odds of Winning Increasing?" *Criminology* 22:551–71.

Menkel-Meadow, Carrie. 1999. "Do the 'Haves' Come Out Ahead in Alternative Judicial Systems? Repeat Players in ADR." *Ohio State Journal on Dispute Resolution* 15:19–61.

Merrett, Chrisopher. 1990. "Detention without Trial in South Africa: The Abuse of Human Rights as State Strategy in the Late 1980s." *Africa Today* 37 (2): 53–66.

Merritt, Deborah Jones, and Kathryn Ann Barry. 1999. "Is the Tort System in Crisis? New Empirical Evidence." *Ohio State Law Journal* 60:315–98.

Miller, Banks, Linda Camp Keith, and Jennifer S. Holmes. 2015. "Leveling the Odds: The Effect of Quality Legal Representation in Cases of Asymmetrical Capability." *Law and Society Review* 49 (1): 209–39.

Miller, Richard E., and Austin Sarat. 1980–1981. "Grievances, Claims, and Disputes: Assessing the Adversary Culture." *Law and Society Review* 15:525–66.

Morton, F. L. 1992. *Pro-Choice Pro-Life: Abortion and the Courts in Canada.* Norman: University of Oklahoma Press.

Moulton, Beatrice A. 1969. "The Persecution and Intimidation of the Low-Income Litigant as Performed by the Small Claims Court in California." *Stanford Law Review* 21:1657.

Muro, S., A. Chehtman, J. S. Mendez, and N. A. Duran. 2018. "Testing Representational Advantage in the Argentine Supreme Court." *Journal of Law and Courts* 6:1–23.

Myers, William M., and Davia C. Downey. 2017. "Which Governments Come Out Ahead?" *Perspectives on Federalism* 9 (1): 13–33.

Nardulli, Peter F. 1986. "'Insider' Justice: Defense Attorneys and the Handling of Felony Cases." *Journal of Criminal Law and Criminology* 77:379–417.

———. 1978. *The Courtroom Elite: An Organization Perspective on Criminal Justice.* Cambridge, MA: Ballinger.

Neustadtl, Alan. 1990. "Interest Group PACmanship: An Analysis of Campaign Contributions, Issue Visibility, and Legislative Impact." *Social Forces* 69:549–64.

O'Connor, Karen. 1980. *Women's Organizations' Use of the Courts.* Lexington, MA: Lexington Books.

O'Connor, Karen, and Lee Epstein. 1983. "The Rise of Conservative Interest Group Litigation." *Journal of Politics* 45:479–89.

———. 1982. "The Importance of Interest Group Involvement in Employment Discrimination Litigation." *Howard Law Journal* 25:709–29.

———. 1981. "Amicus Curiae Participation in U.S. Court Litigation: An Appraisal of Hakman's 'Folklore.'" *Law and Society Review* 16:311–20.

Olson, Susan M. 1990. "Interest-Group Litigation in Federal District Court: Beyond the Political Disadvantage Theory." *Journal of Politics* 52:854–82.

Oppenheimer, David B. 2003. "Verdicts Matter: An Empirical Study of California Employment Discrimination and Wrongful Discharge Jury Verdicts Reveals Low Success Rates for Women and Minorities." *UC Davis Law Review* 37:511–66.

Owen, Harold J. Jr. 1971. "The Role of Trial Courts in the Local Political System: A Comparison of Two Georgia Counties." PhD diss., University of Georgia.

Owens, John E. 1986. "The Impact of Campaign Contributions on Legislative Outcomes in Congress: Evidence from a House Committee." *Political Studies* 34:285–95.

Pagter, C. R., R. McCloskey, and M. Renis. 1964. "The California Small Claims Court." *California Law Review* 52:876.

Palmer, Jan. 1982. "An Econometric Analysis of the U.S. Supreme Court's Certiorari Decisions." *Public Choice* 39:387–98.

Pastore, A., and Maguire, K. 2003. *Sourcebook of Criminal Justice Statistics: 2002.* Washington, DC: US Government Printing Office.

Perry, H. W. Jr. 1991. *Deciding to Decide: Agenda Setting in the United States Supreme Court.* Cambridge, MA: Harvard University Press.

Phillips, Charles David, and Sheldon Ekland-Olson. 1982. "'Repeat Players' in a Criminal Court." *Criminology* 19:530–45.

Pound, Roscoe. 1910. "Law in Books and Law in Action." *Harvard Law Review* 44:12–36.

Priest, G. and B. Klein. 1984. "The Selection of Disputes for Litigation." *Journal of Legal Studies* 13:1–55.

Pritchett, C. Herman. 1948. *The Roosevelt Court: A Study in Judicial Politics and Values 1937–1947.* New York: Macmillan.

Pruitt, Charles R., and James Q. Wilson. 1983. "A Longitudinal Study of the Effect of Race on Sentencing." *Law and Society Review* 17 (4): 613–36.

Quinn, Dennis P., and Robert Y. Shapiro. 1991. "Business Political Power: The Case of Taxation." *American Political Science Review* 85 (3): 851–74.

Reid, Rebecca A., and Todd A. Curry. 2021. "Explaining Indigenous Peoples' success in State Supreme Courts: Party Capability, Judicial Selection, and Representation." *Journal of Law and Courts* 9 (1): 69–87.

Ringquist, Evan J., and Craig E. Emmert. 1999. "Judicial Policymaking in Published and Unpublished Decisions: The Case of Environmental Civil Litigation." *Political Research Quarterly* 52:7–37.

Robbennolt, Jennifer K. 2002. "Determining Punitive Damages: Empirical Insights and Implications for Reform." *Buffalo Law Review* 50:103–203.

Roots, Roger. 2010. "Unfair Federal Rules of Procedure: Why Does the Government Get More Time?" *American Journal of Trial Advocacy* 33:493–520.

Rosenberg, Gerald N. 1991. *The Hollow Hope: Can Courts Bring About Social Change?* Chicago: University of Chicago Press.

Rosenstone, Steven J., and John Mark Hansen. 1993. *Mobilization, Participation, and Democracy in America.* New York: Macmillan.

Rothenberg, Lawrence S. 1992. *Linking Citizens to Government: Interest Group Politics at Common Cause.* New York: Cambridge.

Rousseau, Jean-Jacques. 1768. *Emilius, or, a Treatise of Education. Volume II.* Edinburgh: A. Donaldson.

Rowland, C. K., Robert A. Carp, and Ronald A. Stidham. 1984. "Judges' Policy Choices and the Value Basis of Judicial Appointments: Comparison of Support for Criminal Defendants among Nixon, Johnson, and Kennedy Appointees to the Federal District Courts." *Journal of Politics* 46:886–902.

Rowland, C. K., Donald Songer, and Robert A. Carp. 1988. "Presidential Effects on Criminal Justice Policy in the Lower Federal Courts: The Reagan Judges." *Law and Society Review* 22:191–200.

Ryo, Emily. 2018. "Representing Immigrants: The Role of Lawyers in Immigration Bond Hearings." *Law and Society Review* 52 (2):503–31.

Sahu, Geetanjoy. 2014. "Why the Underdogs Came Out Ahead: An Analysis of the Supreme Court's Environmental Judgments, 1980–2010." *Economic and Political Weekly* 49 (4): 52–58.

Saurette, Paul, and Kelly Gordon. 2015. *The Changing Voice of the Anti-Abortion Movement: The Rise of "Pro-Woman" Rhetoric in Canada and the United States.* Toronto: University of Toronto Press.

Schattschneider, E. E. 1960. *The Semisovereign People: A Realist's View of Democracy in America.* New York: Holt, Rinehart and Winston.

Schlozman, Kay L. 1984. "What Accent the Heavenly Chorus? Political Equality and the American Pressure System." *Journal of Politics* 46 (4): 1006–32.

Schubert, Glendon. 1965. *The Judicial Mind: Attitudes and Ideologies of Supreme Court Justices, 1946–1963.* Evanston, IL: Northwestern University Press

———. 1974. *The Judicial Mind Revisited.* New York: Oxford University Press.

Segal, Jeffrey A. 1988. "Amicus Curiae Briefs by the Solicitor General during the Warren and Burger Courts: A Research Note." *Western Political Quarterly* 41:135–44.

———. 1984. "Predicting Supreme Court Decisions Probabilistically: The Search and Seizure Cases." *American Political Science Review* 78:891–900.

Segal, Jeffrey A., and Albert D. Cover. 1989. "Ideological Values and the Votes of U.S. Supreme Court Justices." *American Political Science Review* 83:557–66.

Segal, Jeffrey A., and Cheryl D. Reedy. 1988. "The Supreme Court and Sex Discrimination: The Role of the Solicitor General." *Western Political Quarterly* 41:553–68.

Segal, Jeffrey, and Harold D. Spaeth. 2002. *The Supreme Court and the Attitudinal Model Revisited.* New York: Cambridge University Press.

———. 1999. *Majority Rule and Minority Will: Adherence to Precedent on the U. S. Supreme Court.* New York: Cambridge University Press.

———. 1996a. "The Influence of Stare Decisis on the Votes of United States Supreme Court Justices." *American Journal of Political Science* 40:971–1003.

———. 1996b. *The Supreme Court and the Attitudinal Model.* New York: Cambridge University Press.

Shaffer, Gregory C. 2009. "How Business Shapes Law: A Socio-Legal Framework." *Connecticut Law Review* 42 (1):147–83.

Shapiro, Martin. 2021. "The Most-Cited Law Scholars Revisited." *University of Chicago Law Review* 88:1595–618.

———. 1981. *Courts: A Comparative and Political Analysis.* Chicago: University of Chicago Press.

Sheehan, Reginald. 1990. "Administrative Agencies and the Court: A Reexamination of the Impact of Agency Type on Decisional Outcomes." *Western Political Quarterly* 43:875–85.

Sheehan, Reginald S., Rebecca D. Gill, and Kirk A. Randazzo. 2012. *Judicialization of Politics: The Interplay of Institutional Structure, Legal Doctrine, and Politics on the High Court of Australia.* Durham, NC: Carolina Academic Press.

Sheehan, Reginald S., William Mishler, and Donald R. Songer. 1992. "Ideology, Status, and the Differential Success of Direct Parties before the Supreme Court." *American Political Science Review* 86:464–71.

Sheehan, Reginald S., and Kirk A. Randazzo. 2012. "Explaining Litigant Success in the High Court of Australia." *Australian Journal of Political Science* 47:239–55.

Shvets, J. 2016. "Presidential Control of the Judiciary via the Appointment Power: Evidence from Russia." *Journal of Law, Economics, and Organization* 32:478–507.

Silberman, Jonathan I., and Garey C. Durden. 1976. "Determining Legislative Preferences on the Minimum Wage: An Economic Approach." *Journal of Political Economy* 84:317–30.

Silliman, G. Sidney. 1981–82. "Dispute Processing by the Philippine Agrarian Court." *Law and Society Review* 16:89–114.

Skiple, J. Kare, Henrik L. Bentsen, and Mark J. McKenzie. 2021. "How Docket Control Shapes Judicial Behavior." *Journal of Law and Courts* 9 (1): 111–36.

Small Claims Study Group. 1972. "Little Injustices: Small Claims Courts and the American Consumer. A Preliminary Report to the Center for Auto Safety." Cambridge, MA.

Smith, Regan G. 1970. "The Small Claims Court: A Sociological Interpretation." PhD diss., University of Illinois.

Smith, Richard A. 1984. "Advocacy, Interpretation, and Influence in the U.S. Congress." *American Political Science Review* 78 (1): 44–63.

Smyth, Russell. 2000. "The 'Haves' and the 'Have Nots': An Empirical Study of the Rational Actor and Party Capability Hypotheses in the High Court 1948–99." *Australian Journal of Political Science* 35:255–74.

Songer, Donald R. 2008. *The Transformation of the Supreme Court of Canada: An Empirical Examination.* Toronto: University of Toronto Press.

Songer, Donald R., Susan W. Johnson, C. L. Ostberg, and Matthew E. Wetstein. 2012. *Law, Ideology, and Collegiality: Judicial Behaviour in the Supreme Court of Canada.* Toronto: McGill-Queen's University Press.

Songer, Donald, Ashlyn Kuersten, and Erin Kaheny. 2000. "Why the Haves Don't Always Come Out Ahead: Repeat Players Meet Amici Curiae for the Disdvantaged." *Political Research Quarterly* 53:537–56.

Songer, Donald R., and Stefanie A. Lindquist. 1996. "Not the Whole Story: The Impact of Justices' Values on Supreme Court Decision Making." *American Journal of Political Science* 40:1049–63.

Songer, Donald R., and Reginald S. Sheehan. 1992. "Who Wins on Appeal? Upperdogs and Underdogs in the United States Courts of Appeals." *American Journal of Political Science* 36:235–58.

Songer, Donald R., Reginald S. Sheehan, and Susan B. Haire. 2003 "Do the "Haves" Come Out Ahead over Time? Applying Galanter's Framework to Decisions of the U.S. Courts of Appeals, 1925–1988." In *In Litigation: Do the "Haves" Still Come Out Ahead?*, ed. Herbert M. Kritzer and Susan Silbey. Stanford: Stanford University Press.

———. 2000. *Continuity and Change on the United States Courts of Appeals.* Ann Arbor: University of Michigan Press.

———. 1999. "Do the "Haves" Come Out Ahead over Time? Applying Galanter's

Framework to Decisions of the U.S. Courts of Appeals, 1925–1988." *Law and Society Review* 33:811–32.

Spohn, Cassia, John Gruhl, and Susan Welch. 1981–82. "The Effect of Race on Sentencing: A Re-Examination of an Unsettled Question." *Law and Society Review* 16:71–88.

Spriggs, James F. II, and Tomas G. Hansford. 2001. "Explaining the Overruling of U.S. Supreme Court Precedent." *Journal of Politics* 63:1091–111.

Spriggs, James F. II, and Paul J. Wahlbeck. 1997. "Amicus Curiae and the Role of Information at the Supreme Court." *Political Research Quarterly* 50:365–86.

Steffensmeier, Darrell, and Stephen Demuth. 2000. "Ethnicity and Sentencing Outcomes in U.S. Federal Courts: Who Is Punished More Harshly?" *American Sociological Review* 65:705–29.

Steffensmeier, Darrell, and Chris Hebert. 1999. "Women and Men Policymakers: Does the Judge's Gender Affect the Sentencing of Criminal Defendants?" *Social Forces* 77:1163–196.

Szmer, John, Susan W. Johnson, and Tammy A. Sarver. 2007. "Does the Lawyer Matter? Influencing Outcomes on the Supreme Court of Canada." *Law and Society Review* 41:279–303.

Szmer, John, Donald R. Songer, and Jennifer Bowie. 2016. "Party Capability and the US Courts of Appeals: Understanding Why the 'Haves' Win." *Journal of Law and Courts* 4 (1): 65–102.

Talesh, Shauhin A. 2014. "Why Marc Galanter's 'Haves' Article Is One of the Most Influential Pieces of Legal Scholarship Ever Written." Foreword to Marc Galanter, *Why the Haves Come Out Ahead: The Classic Essay and New Observations*. New Orleans: Quid Pro Books.

Tate, C. Neal, and Stacia L. Haynie. 1994. "The Philippine Supreme Court under Authoritarian and Democratic Rule: The Perceptions of the Justices." *Asian Profile* 22:209–25.

Toharia, José J. 1975. "Judicial Independence in an Authoritarian Regime: The Case of Contemporary Spain." *Law and Society Review* 9 (3):475–96.

Tauber, Steven C. 1998. "On Behalf of the Condemned? The Impact of the NAACP Legal Defense Fund on Capital Punishment Decision Making in the U. S. Courts of Appeals." *Political Research Quarterly* 51:191–219.

Ulmer, Jeffery T., and Mindy S. Bradley. 2006. "Variation in Trial Penalties among Serious Violent Offenses." *Criminology* 44:631–70.

Ulmer, Sidney S. 1985. "Governmental Litigants, Underdogs, and Civil Liberties in the Supreme Court: 1903–1968 Terms." *Journal of Politics* 47:899–909.

——. 1984. "The Supreme Court's Certiorari Decisions: Conflict as a Predictive Variable." *American Political Science Review* 78:901–11.

Ulmer, Jeffery T., James Eisenstein, and Brian D. Johnson. 2010. "Trial Penalties in Federal Sentencing: Extra-Guidelines Factors and district Variation." *Justice Quarterly* 27 (4):560–92.

Unnever, James D., Charles E. Frazier, and John C. Henretta. 1980. "Race Differences in Criminal Sentencing." *Sociological Quarterly* 21:197–206.

van Koppen, Peter J., and Marijke Malsch. 1991. "Defendants and One-Shotters Win after All: Compliance with Court Decisions in Civil Cases." *Law and Society Review* 25:803–20.

van Zyl Slabbert, Frederick. 1989. "Towards New Strategy Guidelines: Evaluating Conflict Data Trends." *Indicator South Africa* March: 7–20.

Vidmar, N. 1984. "The Small Claims Court: A Reconceptualization of Disputes and an Empirical Investigation." *Law and Society Review* 18:515–50.

Vose, Clement E. 1967. *Caucasians Only: The Supreme Court, the NAACP, and the Restrictive Covenant Cases.* Berkeley: University of California Press.

———. 1966. "Interest Groups, Judicial Review, and Local Government." *Western Political Quarterly* 19:85–100.

Walker, Thomas G., and Deborah J. Barrow. 1985. "The Diversification of the Federal Bench: Policy and Process Ramifications." *Journal of Politics* 47:596–617.

Wanner, Craig. 1974. "The Public Ordering of Private Relations, Part One: Initiating Civil Cases in Urban Trial Courts." *Law and Society Review* 8:421–40.

Welch, W. P. 1982. "Campaign Contributions and Legislative Voting: Milk Money and Dairy Price Supports." *Western Political Quarterly* 35 (4): 478–95.

Wheeler, Stanton, Bliss Cartwright, Robert A. Kagan, and Lawrence M. Friedman. 1987. "Do the 'Haves' Come Out Ahead? Winning and Losing in State Supreme Courts, 1870–1970." *Law and Society Review* 21:403–46.

Wilkins, David B. 1990. "Legal Realism for Layers." *Harvard Law Review* 104:468–524.

Wohlfarth, Patrick C. 2009. "The Tenth Justice? Consequences of Politicization in the Solicitor General's Office." *Journal of Politics* 71 (1): 224–37.

Wu, C. 2019a. "Assessing the Effects of Political Factors on Court Decisions in Corruption Litigation in Taiwan." *Asian Survey* 59 (2): 295–314.

———. 2019b. "Do the 'Haves' Come Out Ahead? Resource Disparity in Public-Land Usurpation Litigation in Taiwan." *Social Science Quarterly* 100:1215–27.

Yarnold, Barbara M. 1995. "Do Courts Respond to the Political Clout of Groups or to Their Superior Litigation Resources/'Repeat Player' Status?" *Justice System Journal* 18:29–42.

Zorn, Christopher J. W. 2002. "U.S. Government Litigation Strategies in the Federal Appellate Courts." *Political Research Quarterly* 55 (1):145–66.

INDEX

In Chambers: Stories of Supreme Court Law Clerks and Their Justices
Todd C. Peppers and Artemus Ward, editors

Merely Judgment: Ignoring, Evading, and Trumping the Supreme Court
Martin J. Sweet

Battle over the Bench: Senators, Interest Groups, and Lower Court Confirmations
Amy Steigerwalt

Law, Politics, and Perception: How Policy Preferences Influence Legal Reasoning
Eileen Braman

The View of the Courts from the Hill: Interactions between Congress and the Federal Judiciary
Mark C. Miller

The Nature of Rights at the American Founding and Beyond
Barry Alan Shain, editor

Strategic Selection: Presidential Nomination of Supreme Court Justices from Herbert Hoover through George W. Bush
Christine L. Nemacheck

Answering the Call of the Court: How Justices and Litigants Set the Supreme Court Agenda
Vanessa A. Baird

Institutional Games and the U.S. Supreme Court
James R. Rogers, Roy B. Flemming, and Jon R. Bond, editors

Judging on a Collegial Court: Influences on Federal Appellate Decision Making
Virginia A. Hettinger, Stefanie A. Lindquist, and Wendy L. Martinek

Justice Curtis in the Civil War Era: At the Crossroads of American Constitutionalism
Stuart Streichler

Creating Constitutional Change: Clashes over Power and Liberty in the Supreme Court
Gregg Ivers and Kevin T. McGuire, editors

Judicial Independence in the Age of Democracy: Critical Perspectives from around the World
Peter H. Russell and David M. O'Brien, editors

Race Relations Litigation in an Age of Complexity
Stephen L. Wasby

www.ingramcontent.com/pod-product-compliance
Lightning Source LLC
Chambersburg PA
CBHW030333270326
41926CB00010B/1604